# LAW ENFORCEMENT CAREER STARTER

# LAW ENFORCEMENT career starter

2nd edition

**Mary Hesalroad**
**with Lauren B. Starkey**

New York

Published in the United States by LearningExpress, LLC, New York.

Library of Congress Cataloging-in-Publication Data:
Hesalroad, Mary.
Law enforcement career starter / Mary Hesalroad with Lauren B. Starkey.—2nd ed.
p. cm.
ISBN 1-57685-364-0
1. Law enforcement—Vocational guidance—United States. 2. Police—Vocational guidance—United States. I. Starkey, Lauren B., 1962– II. Title.

HV8143 .L37 2001
363.2'023'73—dc21 00-046962

Printed in the United States of America
9 8 7 6 5 4 3 2
Second Edition

**Regarding the Information in this Book**
Every effort has been made to ensure accuracy of directory information up until press time. However, phone numbers and/or addresses are subject to change. Please contact the respective organization for the most recent information.

**For Further Information**
For information on LearningExpress, other LearningExpress products, or bulk sales, please write to us at:

LearningExpress™
900 Broadway
Suite 604
New York, NY 10003

Or visit our website at:
www.learnatest.com

# About the Authors

**Mary Hesalroad,** author of the first edition, is a former police officer with over eight years of experience. She is now a writer and law enforcement consultant living in Austin, Texas.

**Lauren B. Starkey** is a developmental editor living in Essex Junction, Vermont.

# Contents

# Introduction

**THE FIRST** edition of this book noted that the U.S. Department of Labor estimated that opportunities in law enforcement fields would continue to grow faster than average through the year 2005. Now, a few years later, the Department of Labor is just as optimistic. Their Bureau of Labor Statistics projects that faster-than-average growth will continue through 2008. This is great news to those who are considering a career in law enforcement.

It is important to note, however, that although jobs are plentiful, the competition is stiff. Police departments and other agencies are actually setting stricter standards for their recruits. Since it can cost over $60,000 to hire, train, and equip a new officer, no one wants to make the mistake of hiring someone who won't be able to make it in their chosen profession.

You should also know that there are thousands of law enforcement agencies throughout the country, and they differ from one another in important ways. For instance, some require you to take a test as part of the application process, while others don't; some ask for a resume, and others won't accept them. Some police departments allow you to apply for a job right out of high school, while others won't accept your application until after college graduation.

This book is designed to help you negotiate the often confusing field of law enforcement. In Chapter 1, you will get an overview of the field. It will explore the risks, rewards (including salaries and benefits), requirements, and responsibilities of police work. A suitability test at the end of the chapter may help you to see if you have the personality traits most often associated with successful law enforcement personnel.

Chapter 2 is about your education: specifically, how much and what kind you may need to apply for a job in law enforcement. There is also information to help you find the right school, and even how to pay for it once you get in. Law enforcement internships and fields of study are also explained. Finally, you will get advice and comments from those working in the field.

You may want to consider, or already are considering, joining the military if you are planning a career in law enforcement. Chapter 3 details the advantages of military service; it also explains the five branches that make up the military, the four routes to the military, and how military service can help to pay for your education.

Chapters 4 and 5 explore many of the hundreds of law enforcement jobs that exist at local, state, and federal levels. You will find descriptions of the jobs, qualifications, selections processes, and training. There are resources to guide you to job openings for many of these positions, as well as advice on how to use the Internet in your job search. Advice from those already working in a variety of law enforcement careers may be found throughout these chapters. As mentioned above, you will be faced with stiff competition. Even those jobs that seem less desirable, because of low pay and/or harsh working conditions, receive responses from more individuals than they can hire. In Chapter 6, you will learn how to successfully market your skills and experience to future employers, so you can be the competition to beat. The law enforcement hiring process is examined in detail, so you won't be surprised by anything along the way.

Finally, Appendices A, B, and C, are designed to lead you to even more sources that can help you with your career search. Appendix A focuses on the Internet as the most important tool for getting the current information you need, from scholarship and internship listings, to online application forms for many jobs. Appendix B lists all of the field offices for the Federal Bureau of Investigation (FBI)—one of the country's largest federal employers of law enforcement personnel. In Appendix C, you will find a variety of books and other publications that can further assist you.

Every effort has been made to make this book as user-friendly as possible, giving you all the information you need to start your career in law enforcement—in one place. Although it can be a difficult process, your search can end exactly where you want it to—with you employed in the law enforcement job you desire.

# CHAPTER one

## CHOOSING A CAREER IN LAW ENFORCEMENT

THIS CHAPTER will give you an overview of law enforcement work. We will examine the requirements and responsibilities of jobs in the field, as well as average salaries and benefits. You will also learn about the risks of these jobs, and find out the general personality traits hiring agencies look for in new recruits. Finally, there is a test at the end to help you determine if you are suited for this challenging career.

**ACCORDING TO** the Bureau of Labor Statistics, employment of police officers and detectives is expected to increase faster than the average for all occupations through 2008. They note that "a more security-conscious society and concern about drug-related crimes should contribute to the increasing demand for police services." This is encouraging news to anyone interested in a career in law enforcement.

By using this book, you will get a better idea whether or not your interest can translate into a future career. If you already know you want to go into law enforcement, but you aren't sure about which of the hundreds of actual job opportunities is best for you, turn to Chapters 4 and 5 for detailed information about many of them. If police work in general interests you, but you aren't sure about the risks and rewards of this work, read on. While they vary somewhat from position to position, for much of the field the requirements are the same.

## TYPICAL SALARIES AND BENEFITS

Before taking a job in any field, you will need to decide on your own salary requirements. Do you live in a big city and plan to stay there? Are you willing to relocate to a less-expensive suburb or rural area? Do you have a family that you must support? Are you paying off student loans? No matter how much you enjoy your work, your job will need to meet your salary requirements in order for you to stay with it.

### Local and State

With law enforcement work, there is a large pay range. According to the Bureau of Labor Statistics, police officers earned an average of $37,710 in 1998. Sheriffs and deputy sheriffs had a median annual salary that year of $28,270, and detectives and criminal investigators earned an average of $46,180. But if you consider overtime pay, which can be significant, and the many benefits offered to law enforcement personnel, these numbers may reach much higher.

**JUST THE FACTS**

The first American system of law enforcement was established in Boston in 1631. It was called the Night Watch, and its officers worked part-time, and received no pay.

Because police departments hire more officers than any other type of law enforcement agency, they are worth a closer look. The box below gives more specific information for some of the largest agencies in the country. Remember that salaries do not include additional money that can be earned for working overtime, on hazardous duty, or on less desirable shifts (taking the night shift can earn bonus pay). Many departments also add to your base pay after you have completed police academy training or finished a probationary period (usually your first year on the job). It is also possible to earn more each year for education: having a college degree (or even some college credit) or getting advanced certification relating to your law enforcement work can mean extra income each year, depending on where you work. (See Chapter 2 for more information on educational incentive pay.)

### BALTIMORE POLICE DEPARTMENT

www.ci.baltimore.md.us/government/police

Average yearly salary: $28,404–40,029

Benefits include: health insurance; life insurance; paid vacation, holidays, and sick leave; uniform allowance; tuition reimbursement; pension plan; retirement after 20 years

### BOSTON POLICE DEPARTMENT

www.ci.boston.ma.us/police

Average yearly salary: $40,000 after three years

Benefits include: paid vacation; pension plan; tuition reimbursement

### CHICAGO POLICE DEPARTMENT

www.ci.chi.il.us/CommunityPolicing

Average yearly salary: $33,522

Benefits include: health insurance; paid vacation and sick leave; pension plan; tuition reimbursement

### DALLAS POLICE DEPARTMENT

www.ci.dallas.tx.us/dpd

Average starting salary: $28,498–29,919

Benefits include: health insurance; life insurance; paid vacation and sick leave

### LOS ANGELES POLICE DEPARTMENT

www.lapdonline.org/index/htm

Average yearly salary: $41,175–55,311

Benefits include: health insurance; paid vacation and sick leave; pension plan

### MIAMI-DADE POLICE DEPARTMENT

www.mdpd.metro-dade.com

Average starting salary: $31,300

Benefits include: health insurance; life insurance; paid vacation; tuition reimbursement; pension plan

### NEW YORK CITY POLICE DEPARTMENT

www.ci.nyc.ny.us/html/nypd/home.html

Average starting salary: $34,970 (includes uniform allowance, holiday pay, and night shift differential)

Benefits include: health insurance; pension plan; tuition reimbursement

### PHILADELPHIA POLICE DEPARTMENT

www.phila.gov/departments/police

Average starting salary: $28,511

Benefits include: health insurance; life insurance; paid vacation and sick leave; uniform allowance; pension plan

### SAN FRANCISCO POLICE DEPARTMENT

www.ci.sf.ca.us/police

Average yearly salary: $48,300

Benefits include: health insurance; paid sick leave and vacation; uniform allowance; pension plan

### WASHINGTON, D.C. POLICE DEPARTMENT

www.mpdc.org/English/Recruiting/PoliceOfficer.htm

Average starting salary: $25,872

Benefits include: health insurance; life insurance; paid vacation and sick leave; pension plan

In addition to pension plans and deferred-income savings (where you can put away money every month before paying taxes on it, as savings for retirement), most police departments will pay at least half of your salary for the rest of your life after retirement (as few as 20 years after your hiring date). For instance, the New York City Police Department pays 50% after 20 years, Portland Police Department pays 84% after 30 years, and Orlando Police pays 80% after 25 years.

Corrections Departments around the country offer benefits similar to those of state and local police, but salaries tend to be lower. For instance, a corrections officer in Texas earns about $27,000, 20 months after being hired. A police officer in Dallas makes more than that as a starting salary. In Washington state, a corrections officer starts at $25,872, while a police officer in Seattle averages $38,508–40,524. Check Chapter 4 for more information about law enforcement positions at the state and local levels.

## Federal Salaries

Job openings for most federal positions are listed with the Office of Personnel Management (OPM). Government jobs almost all follow the general pay schedule, on which you can look up a job by its level, called a "grade," and find out the salary. Within each grade there are pay increases, called "steps," which are also listed on the pay schedule. Law enforcement officers have their own government pay schedule (see the chart on page 6 or check out the complete schedules at www.opm.gov/oca/2000tbls). Hiring levels are always part of a government job listing, so it is important to read carefully, noting, for instance, that FBI agents are hired at GS-10, while Secret Service Agents are hired at GS-5. If you have extra qualifications, such as experience in the scientific, medical, or technical fields, you may be hired at a higher level. A detailed explanation of the OPM and federal job listings is found in Chapter 5.

As with state and local jobs, base pay is adjusted at the federal level once you have completed training and received your first assignment. There is also something called "locality payment," which is added to your salary based on where your job takes you. The government determines which cities cost more or are less desirable to live in, then they adjust base pay accordingly. If you are assigned to an area of the country that has not received special consideration, a rate of 6.78% is added to your pay (this rate is reflected in the chart on page 6). Atlanta, Georgia has a 7.66% locality payment, while New York and northern New Jersey have one of 16%.

## Salary Table 2000-RUS (LEO)

Rates of Pay for Law Enforcement Officers,
Including Special Salary Rates at GS-3 through GS-10 and Incorporating the 3.8% General Schedule Increase
and a Locality Payment of 6.78% for the Locatlity Pay Area of Rest of U.S.(Net Increase: 4.69%)
Effective January 2000
Annual Rates by Grade and Step

| | 1 | 2 | 3 | 4 | 5 | 6 | 7 | 8 | 9 | 10 |
|---|---|---|---|---|---|---|---|---|---|---|
| GS-1 | $14,810 | $15,304 | $15,797 | $16,286 | $16,780 | $17,070 | $17,555 | $18,046 | $18,065 | $18,527 |
| 2 | 16,651 | 17,046 | 17,598 | 18,065 | 18,267 | 18,804 | 19,341 | 19,878 | 20,415 | 20,952 |
| 3 | 21,801 | 22,407 | 23,012 | 23,618 | 24,223 | 24,828 | 25,434 | 26,039 | 26,645 | 27,250 |
| 4 | 24,476 | 25,156 | 25,836 | 26,517 | 27,197 | 27,877 | 28,557 | 29,237 | 29,918 | 30,598 |
| 5 | 28,141 | 28,901 | 29,661 | 30,422 | 31,182 | 31,942 | 32,702 | 33,463 | 34,223 | 34,983 |
| 6 | 29,674 | 30,522 | 31,370 | 32,218 | 33,065 | 33,913 | 34,761 | 35,609 | 36,457 | 37,305 |
| 7 | 32,032 | 32,974 | 33,915 | 34,857 | 35,799 | 36,741 | 37,683 | 38,624 | 38,566 | 40,508 |
| 8 | 33,389 | 34,432 | 35,476 | 36,519 | 37,562 | 38,605 | 39,648 | 40,692 | 41,735 | 42,778 |
| 9 | 35,728 | 36,880 | 38,032 | 39,184 | 40,336 | 41,488 | 42,640 | 43,793 | 44,945 | 46,097 |
| 10 | 39,345 | 40,615 | 41,884 | 43,154 | 44,424 | 45,693 | 46,963 | 48,233 | 49,502 | 50,772 |
| 11 | 41,834 | 43,229 | 44,623 | 46,018 | 47,412 | 48,807 | 50,202 | 51,596 | 52,991 | 54,385 |
| 12 | 50,139 | 51,810 | 53,481 | 55,152 | 56,823 | 58,494 | 60,165 | 61,836 | 63,507 | 65,179 |
| 13 | 59,623 | 61,610 | 63,597 | 65,584 | 67,571 | 69,559 | 71,546 | 73,533 | 75,520 | 77,507 |
| 14 | 70,457 | 72,805 | 75,153 | 77,501 | 79,849 | 82,197 | 84,545 | 86,893 | 89,241 | 91,589 |
| 15 | 82,876 | 85,639 | 88,401 | 91,163 | 93,926 | 96,688 | 99,451 | 102,213 | 104,975 | 107,738 |

## Entry Level Basic Pay by Occupation

| Occupation | Starting Salary |
|---|---|
| FBI Special Agent | $39,345 |
| Secret Service Special Agent | $28,141; $32,032; $35,728* |
| Secret Service Uniformed Division Officer | $34,879 |
| AFT Special Agent | $28,141 |
| Bureau of Prisons, Correctional Officer | $22,819; $25,435* |

*rate offered depends on your qualifications

## RISKS

Law enforcement work is not without risks. The injury rate among officers and agents is higher than in many other occupations, for obvious reasons. Few other jobs may start the day with a high-speed car chase or end it taking drugs away from people who don't want to give them up. Even when law enforcement professionals aren't directly in harm's way, they often have to perform duties that are difficult or disturbing, such as dealing with bloody accident scenes or interviewing victims of sexual assault.

Dr. Rick Bradstreet, a police psychiatrist for over 19 years, suggests checking out the law enforcement career you want before taking the job:

> Police work isn't the same as deputy sheriff's work, and deputy's work is not like DPS (state troopers) work. Go ride with officers in the area that you want to work. Get exposed to the work and talk to people about the real ups and downs. We've had people quit after seeing fatal auto accidents—one cadet saw a bloody bar fight and quit. They weren't exposed enough to the work to see that this isn't the job they wanted.

Being exposed to risks on a daily basis leads to stress. It comes from coping with everything from angry motorists to nasty weather; from dealing with citizens who believe that all law enforcement officials are corrupt or racist, to dealing with the stress of not knowing what's going to happen next during a shift. And since cops, deputies, and federal agents are all human, there is a tendency to bring work-related problems home, which can sometimes lead to trouble with family relationships. Many law enforcement agencies help their employees by offering benefits such as generous amounts of paid sick leave and free personal and family counseling.

## LAW ENFORCEMENT WORK DAY-TO-DAY

There are certainties of law enforcement work that apply to just about any position, whether you are employed as a patrol officer or as a special agent with the U.S. Customs Service. The first certainty is rotating shifts. Don't expect to work nine-to-five, five days a week. Instead, you will most likely have rotating days off; you'll work nights, weekends, and holidays; and overtime pay is standard.

You should also consider that you need to be strong, both physically and emotionally. Officers and agents need to be in excellent shape because you may need to be on your feet for hours at a time, the weather may be bad, and self-defense can be necessary. Strength of character is a crucial characteristic of good law enforcement professionals. In this line of work, you must have a highly developed sense of responsibility and respect for authority. You'll need to be fair and open-minded, honest, even-tempered, tactful, quick-thinking, disciplined, and self-confident. You must be able to make decisions independently, cope with high levels of stress, and exercise sound judgment.

The Los Angeles Police Department hired the first policewoman in America in 1910. Alice Stebbin Wells entered the force at the rank of detective. Five years later, she founded the International Association of Policewomen.

You also have to be good at handling people. Law enforcement is all about people—their actions and reactions. You'll serve citizens who have different beliefs and who come from different backgrounds, citizens of all races, religions, gender, sexual preference, age, and socioeconomic levels. No matter what form your private beliefs may take, you must treat all people equally and fairly under the law. Sheriff Don Farley, of the Rockingham County Sheriff's Office in Virginia, believes:

> Being an officer is much like being an umpire in a game. No matter what decision you make, someone is going to be upset. An officer must be able to interpret the law so that the people involved have an understanding about the action you have taken.

Good oral and written communication skills are a must. Law enforcement involves constant communication, whether it's with fellow officers, dispatchers, victims, witnesses, or suspects. You must be able to express yourself in an appropriate, effective manner. The ability to write clearly and concisely is important since you will have to write reports that may become legal evidence in a court case.

Your observation skills must be keen. Your ability to notice and remember telling details is highly important when conducting an investigation. This ability is especially useful when you sit down to write your report and when you testify in court cases. It is the skill you need most to alert you to suspicious behavior.

You will need a good memory. It is important to honestly assess this skill now, and work on it if you have a weakness. Some people remember names well but can't put them with the right faces. Others forget names quickly but know exactly when, where, and why they met the person whose name they've forgotten. If you don't think you have a good memory, you can develop one. It is a skill that improves with practice.

## Many Choices

As you will learn in the chapters ahead, there are hundreds of different types of law enforcement careers available. You can become part of a K-9 unit and work with specially trained police dogs; you can fly a helipcopter for the Immigration and Naturalization Service; you can serve an entire small community as its one-person police force. If you have an interest in technology, you may be able to specialize in such areas as forensic science or polygraph testing. Many law enforcement agencies are looking for those who have computer experience, as they use them to combat crime. Computer crime itself is a relatively new area with great growth opportunity; as more and more people use the Internet, more and more crimes are committed there. Don't limit your thinking about your future career at this stage—learn about the great variety of choices in the field of law enforcement.

## IN THE NEWS

**Fighting Cyber Crimes**

As the Internet brings more and more useful information to students, business people, homemakers, and retirees, it is also becoming the site of more and more crime. You can research a report on dinosaurs, check the stock market, find out how to make explosives, and view images of child pornography. Law enforcement agencies are now struggling with how best to "police" the Internet.

The University of Iowa Public Safety Department expects that it will soon be dealing with cybercrime daily, so it is sending its officials to week-long seminars during 2000 to learn how to deal with it. To address the problem of "anonymous" criminals, they are finding out how to track suspicious e-mails by using information found in their headers. Once a cyber criminal is caught, though, law enforcement officials have to use laws that were not written to deal with cybercrimes.

## The Hiring Process

In order to be hired by a law enforcement agency, you will have to go through a selection process that can take anywhere from several months to a year or more. Why such a long and complicated process? Because law enforcement work—as police officer, state trooper, federal agent, or corrections officer—is difficult. Whether you're patrolling a beat, the highways, or a cell block, you need a lot of positive character traits, life experience, and skills, and the agency you want to work for needs to know that you are qualified.

In most areas, many more people apply for law enforcement positions than can ever be accepted. For instance, thousands of applicants applied to the Portland Police Department in 1997, but only a hundred or so made the grade. The hiring process involves a series of steps that must be passed before an agency can put someone on its eligibility list; a large percentage of people who apply fail one or more of these steps.

Chapter 6 of this book details specifically the steps of the hiring process. Reading it carefully, and following the expert advice given, can help you to negotiate this process successfully.

## THE POLICE OFFICER SUITABILITY TEST

The following self-evaluation quiz can help you decide whether you and a career in law enforcement will make a good match. There is no one "type" of person who becomes a police officer; they are as varied as any other group of people in their personalities, experiences, and styles. At the same time, there are some attitudes and behaviors that predict success and satisfaction in this profession. They have nothing to do with your intelligence or ability; they simply reflect how you interact with other people and how you choose to approach the world.

These "suitability factors" were pulled from research literature and discussions with police psychologists and screeners across the country. The factors fall into five groups; each has ten questions spaced throughout this test.

The LearningExpress Police Officer Suitability Test is not a formal psychological test. For one thing, it's not long enough: the MMPI (Minnesota Multiphasic Personality Inventory) test used in most psychological assessments has 11 times more items than you'll find here. In addition, it does not focus on your general mental health.

Instead, the test should be viewed as an informal guide, a private tool to help you decide whether being a police officer would suit you and whether you would enjoy it. It also provides the opportunity for greater self-understanding, which is beneficial no matter what you do for a living.

### Directions

You will need about 20 minutes to answer the 50 questions below. It's a good idea to do them all at one sitting—scoring and interpretation can be done later. For each question, consider how often the attitude or behavior applies to you. You have a choice between Never, Rarely, Sometimes, Often, and Always. Put the number for your answer in the space after each question. For example, if the answer is "sometimes," the score for that item is 10; "always" scores a 40, and so on. How they add up will be explained later. If you try to outsmart the test or figure out the "right" answers, you won't get an accurate picture. Just be honest.

PLEASE NOTE: Don't read the scoring sections before you answer the questions, or you will defeat the whole purpose of the exercise!

How often do the following statements sound like you? Choose one answer for each statement.

| NEVER | RARELY | SOMETIMES | OFTEN | ALWAYS |
|---|---|---|---|---|
| 0 | 5 | 10 | 20 | 40 |

1. I like to know what's expected of me. ____
2. I am willing to admit my mistakes to other people. ____
3. Once I've made a decision, I stop thinking about it. ____
4. I can shrug off my fears about getting physically hurt. ____
5. I like to know what to expect. ____
6. It takes a lot to get me really angry. ____
7. My first impressions of people tend to be accurate. ____
8. I am aware of my stress level. ____
9. I like to tell other people what to do. ____
10. I enjoy working with others. ____
11. I trust my instincts. ____
12. I enjoy being teased. ____
13. I will spend as much time as it takes to settle a disagreement. ____
14. I feel comfortable in new social situations. ____
15. When I disagree with people, I let them know about it. ____
16. I'm in a good mood. ____
17. I'm comfortable making quick decisions when necessary. ____
18. Rules must be obeyed, even if you don't agree with them. ____
19. I like to say exactly what I mean. ____
20. I enjoy being with people. ____
21. I stay away from doing exciting things that I know are dangerous. ____

22. I don't mind when a boss tells me what to do.____
23. I enjoy solving puzzles. ____
24. The people I know consult me about their problems. ____
25. I am comfortable making my own decisions. ____
26. People know where I stand on things. ____
27. When I get stressed, I know how to make myself relax. ____
28. I have confidence in my own judgment. ____
29. I make my friends laugh. ____
30. When I make a promise, I keep it. ____
31. When I'm in a group, I tend to be the leader. ____
32. I can deal with sudden changes in my routine. ____
33. When I get into a fight, I can stop myself from losing control. ____
34. I am open to new facts that might change my mind. ____
35. I understand why I do the things I do. ____
36. I'm good at calming people down. ____
37. I can tell how people are feeling even when they don't say anything. ____
38. I take criticism without getting upset. ____
39. People follow my advice. ____
40. I pay attention to people's body language. ____
41. It's important for me to make a good impression. ____
42. I remember to show up on time. ____
43. When I meet new people, I try to understand them. ____
44. I avoid doing things on impulse. ____
45. Being respected is important to me. ____
46. People see me as a calm person. ____
47. It's more important for me to do a good job than to get praised for it. ____
48. I make my decisions based on common sense. ____
49. I prefer to keep my feelings to myself when I'm with strangers. ____
50. I take responsibility for my own actions rather than blame others. ____

### Scoring

Attitudes and behaviors can't be measured in units, like distance or weight. As a result, the numbers and dividing lines between score ranges are approximate, and numbers may vary about 20 points either way. If your score doesn't fall in the optimal range, it doesn't indicate a "failure"—only an area that needs focus.

It may help to share your test results with people who are close to you. Very often, there are differences between how we see ourselves and how we actually come across to others. You may gain a more accurate assessment of your strengths and weaknesses by taking the test, and then discussing the outcome with those who know you well.

## GROUP 1—RISK

Add up scores for questions 4, 6, 12, 15, 21, 27, 33, 38, 44, and 46.

**Total =** ____

This group evaluates your tendency to be assertive and take risks. The ideal is in the middle, somewhere between timid and reckless: you should be willing to take risks, but not seek them out just for excitement. Being nervous, impulsive, and afraid of physical injury are all undesirable traits for a police officer. This group also reflects how well you take teasing and criticism, both of which you may encounter every day. And as you can imagine, it is vitally important for someone who carries a gun not to have a short fuse.

- A score between 360 and 400 is extreme, suggesting a "macho" approach that could be dangerous in the field.
- If you score between 170 and 360, you are on the right track.
- If you score between 80 and 170, you may want to think about how comfortable you are with the idea of confrontation.
- A score between 0 and 80 indicates that the more dangerous and stressful aspects of the job might be difficult for you.

## GROUP 2—CORE

Add up scores for questions 2, 8, 16, 19, 26, 30, 35, 42, 47, and 50

**Total =** ____

This group reflects such basic traits as stability, reliability, and self-awareness. Can your fellow officers count on you to back them up and do your part? Are you secure enough to do your job without needing praise? In the words of one police psychologist, "If you're hungry for praise, you will starve to death." The public will not always appreciate your efforts, and your supervisors and colleagues may be too busy or preoccupied to pat you on the back.

It is crucial to be able to admit your mistakes and take responsibility for your actions, to be confident without being arrogant or conceited, and to be straightforward and direct in your communication. In a job where lives are at stake, the facts must be clear. Mood is also very important. While we all have good and bad days, someone who is depressed much of the time is not encouraged to pursue police work; depression affects one's judgment, energy level, and ability to respond and communicate.

- If you score between 180 and 360, you're in the ballpark.
- 360+ may be unrealistic.
- A score of 100–180 indicates you should look at the questions again and re-evaluate your style of social interaction.
- Scores between 0 and 100 suggest you may not be ready for this job—yet.

## GROUP 3—JUDGMENT

Add scores for questions 3, 7, 11, 17, 23, 28, 37, 40, 43, and 48.

**Total =** ____

This group reveals how you make decisions. Successful police officers are sensitive to unspoken messages, can detect and respond to other people's feelings, and make fair and accurate assessments of a situation, rather than being influenced by their own personal biases and needs. Once the decision to act is made, second-guessing can be dangerous. Police officers must make their best judgments in line with accepted practices, and then act upon these judgments without hesitancy or self-doubt. Finally, it's important to know and accept that you cannot change the world single-handedly. People who seek this career because they want to make a dramatic individual difference in human suffering are likely to be frustrated and disappointed.

- A score over 360 indicates you may be trying too hard.
- If you scored between 170 and 360, your style of making decisions, especially about people, fits with the desired police officer profile.
- Scores between 80 and 170 suggest that you think about how you make judgments and how much confidence you have in them.
- If you scored less than 170, making judgments may be a problem area for you.

## GROUP 4—AUTHORITY

Add scores for questions 1, 10, 13, 18, 22, 25, 31, 34, 39, and 45.

**Total** = ____

This group contains the essential attributes of respect for rules and authority—including the "personal authority" of self-reliance and leadership—and the ability to resolve conflict and work with a team. Again, a good balance is the key. Police officers must accept and communicate the value of structure and control without being rigid. And even though most decisions are made independently in the field, the authority of the supervisor and the law must be obeyed at all times. Anyone on a personal mission for justice or vengeance will not make a good police officer and is unlikely to make it through the screening process.

- A score between 160 and 360 indicates you have the desired attitude toward authority—both your own and that of your superior officers. Any higher is a bit extreme.
- If you scored between 100 and 160, you might think about whether a demanding leadership role is something you want every day.
- With scores between 0 and 100, ask yourself whether the required combination of structure and independence would be comfortable for you.

## GROUP 5—STYLE

Add up scores for questions 5, 9, 14, 20, 24, 29, 32, 36, 41, and 49.

**Total** = ____

This is the personal style dimension, which describes how you come across to others. Moderation rules here as well: police officers should be seen as strong and capable, but not dramatic or heavy-handed; friendly, but not overly concerned with whether they are liked; patient, but not to the point of losing control of a situation. A good sense of humor is essential, not only in the field but among one's fellow officers. Flexibility is another valuable trait—especially given all the changes that can happen in one shift—but too much flexibility can be perceived as weakness.

- A score between 160 and 360 is optimal. Over 360 is trying too hard.
- Scores between 80 and 160 suggest that you compare your style with the description above and consider whether anything needs to be modified.

- If you scored between 0 and 80, you might think about the way you interact with others and whether you'd be happy in a job where people are the main focus.

## Summary

The Police Officer Suitability Test reflects the fact that being a successful police officer requires moderation rather than extremes. Attitudes that are desirable in reasonable amounts can become a problem if they are too strong. For example, independence is a necessary trait, but too much of it creates a "Dirty Harry" type who takes the law into his or her own hands. Going outside accepted police procedure is a bad idea; worse, it can put other people's lives in jeopardy.

As one recruiter said, the ideal police officer is "low key and low maintenance." In fact, there's only one thing you can't have too much of, and that's common sense. With everything else, balance is the key. Keep this in mind as you look at your scores.

This test was developed by Judith Schlesinger, Ph.D., a writer and psychologist whose background includes years of working with police officers in psychiatric crisis interventions.

### THE INSIDE TRACK

**Who:** Michael Berkow
**What:** Chief of Police
**Where:** South Pasadena, California, Police Department
**How long:** 3 years
**Degree:** Bachelor's degree, Kalamazoo College, Michigan; Master's degree, Johns Hopkins University, Baltimore; Law degree, Syracuse University College of Law

I was always interested in public service and public safety. Before I went to college, I was a fire department Explorer and then a volunteer. In college, I worked with several police and fire agencies. After graduation, I applied to police departments in New York, Boston, Philadelphia, and Chicago. The only one hiring was in Rochester, New York. I had to take the civil service exam, and score well to get hired. In agencies that use the test, your score is the most important part of the process. It doesn't matter what your abilities or education are if you don't score well.

Since that first job, I have worked for the U.S. Department of Justice as a police project manager in charge of International Police Projects. I ran the program to create the first civilian police force in Haiti, and the U.S. Police Program to rebuild the Somali force. I was also chief of police in Coachella, California. This department needed a lot of work; it is in a very poor city, with a very high crime rate, including a lot of violent crime.

A chief of police sits on a three-legged stool. These legs are the community, the political/professional leadership of your city (your boss), and your employees. It is important to recognize each group and to work with each. You want to try to keep the stool balanced, which can be a tough thing to do.

My advice to anyone interested in a law enforcement career is to start early. You need to start thinking about your ethics and making tough choices at an early age, when many of your peers are not. Later, you will be asked about drug use, drinking, vandalism, and stealing. You can't be involved in these things if you want to be a cop. Remember that anything you do becomes part of your package forever.

I would also suggest joining the Police Explorers or getting a part-time job as a Police Cadet, so you can see police work and get your hands dirty. You could also volunteer at a training center to be a role player for police trainees, or go to your local police department and ask for a ride-along.

# CHAPTER two

## BECOMING A CANDIDATE: YOUR EDUCATION

THIS CHAPTER is designed to help you make crucial education decisions before you apply for a job in law enforcement. You will learn why college is fast becoming a recruiting requirement of many agencies, how to find the right school, and even how to pay for it once you get it. Law enforcement internships and fields of study will also be covered. Finally, you will get advice and comments from those working in the field.

**WITH TOUGHER** hiring standards in place, recruiters are looking for candidates who not only meet their requirements, but who really stand out. The following two chapters will explore a number of ways in which you can become the stand-out candidate. We will start with arguably the most important thing you can bring with you as you start your career—a good education.

### WHY COLLEGE?

In 1967, the President's Crime Commission recommended that the goal of police agencies should be to have every officer hold a bachelor's degree.

Although this goal hasn't been met, it is true that more education is expected from candidates than ever before, and the trend continues to grow. Frank Marousek, Assistant Dean of Admissions for John Jay College, thinks law enforcement and higher education are joining forces across the United States:

> I think the days of graduating high school or getting a GED and then going right into law enforcement are just about gone. Many police agencies in the nation require college credit or a degree as a prerequisite for appointment.

While requirements vary from a four-year college degree for many federal agencies (including the FBI) to a high-school or General Equivalency Diploma (GED) for police departments such as Seattle, Washington, and Ventura County, California, it is clear that the more education you have, the more attractive you will be as a candidate for a job in law enforcement. A Police Executive Research Forum study of almost 700 police departments found that while only 14 percent of the departments require some college, the national average for police officers' education is high school plus two years of college. And the number of departments requiring two or more years of college education is on the rise.

Louis A. Mayo, founder and director of the Police Association for College Education (PACE), notes that the Portland, Oregon, Tulsa, Oklahoma, and Charleston, South Carolina police departments, as well as the Illinois State Police have all recently instituted a requirement of a four-year college degree for applicants. The bottom line, according to Mayo, is that "if you want to be a successful police officer, you should get a four-year college degree."

College-educated applicants stand out to a recruiter in a number of ways. The recruiter can safely assume that they made a commitment and were responsible enough to show up for classes and to study hard enough to pass final exams. They listened to lectures, participated in class discussions and projects, read books, wrote papers, and took tests—all of which improved their communication and problem-solving skills. So, when looking to hire people who are likely to make it through page after page of state, local, or federal laws; write coherent, informative reports, and communicate well with a variety of people, it is clear why agencies lean toward candidates with proven track records. Law enforcement recruiters also know that applicants who've had college experience are going to be better equipped to handle growth and change as law enforcement becomes more and more sophisticated in its strategies, methods, and technologies.

To add to the incentives for obtaining a college degree, there may be financial rewards for your education. Many law enforcement agencies, especially police departments, are willing to increase your salary for college hours and/or degrees. Police employers may add a bonus to starting base salaries, usually after you successfully complete academy training. The chart below gives a few examples of how education can pay off. The numbers in the "Bonus Pay Added to Base" column is how much extra they add to your base salary in return for the number of college hours you earned or the kind of degree you have.

| Department | College Hours or Degree | Bonus Pay Added to Base |
|---|---|---|
| Albuquerque Police Dept. (NM) | 4-year | $1620 per year |
| Atlanta Police Dept. (GA) | 2-year | $1275 per year |
| | 4-year | $2551 per year |
| Dallas Police Dept. (TX) | 90 hrs | $720 per year |
| | 4-year | $1200 per year |
| Indianapolis Police Dept. (IN) | 30 hrs | $250 per year |
| | 60 hrs | $500 per year |
| | 90 hrs | $750 per year |
| | 4-year | $1000 per year |
| Lexington Police Dept. (KY) | up to 59 hrs | $400 per year |
| | up to 89 hrs | $700 per year |
| | up to 119 hrs | $900 per year |
| Newport News Police Dept. (VA) | 2-year | $600 per year |
| | 4-year | $1000 per year |
| Orlando Police Dept. (FL) | 2-year | $360 per year |
| | 4-year | $960 per year |

As if financial incentive wasn't enough, consider that you might need a college education to get promoted from lower level jobs. For instance, the New

York City Police Department requires 64 college credits to advance to the rank of sergeant, 90 credits for lieutenant, and a bachelor's degree for captain. The San Diego Police Department requires two years of college for sergeants. Your best chance to stay competitive for the best jobs and promotions in law enforcement is to get a quality education. Dean Marousek agrees:

> It bodes well for anyone to go to college first, or go to college while they are working or while they are in the military. You are going to need it eventually. Here in the New York City Police Department, if you want to be promoted you have to have at least 60 credits. The level of education you need increases as you go up the ranks.

## FIELDS OF STUDY

If you have decided that you need a two- or four-year degree before or during your pursuit of a career in law enforcement, the next step is to consider what you will study and to what schools you should apply. Many colleges and universities across the country have criminal justice degree programs. The best way to locate them is to consult one or several college guides, many of which are listed later in the chapter. However, you don't necessarily need to major in one of these programs.

There are many in the field who believe that a well-rounded college education, one that includes courses in accounting, psychology, foreign languages, and those that will improve your communication and computer skills, makes for the best candidate. You can concentrate your study on any one of these areas and enhance your skills needed for your future career. The Berkeley, California, police department, for example, requires sixty college credits, and specifies that they be in administration of justice, criminology, police science, public administration, psychology, sociology, and/or English.

If you do decide to get a bachelor's degree in criminal justice, you will need 33 credits in your major, which might look like this:

| | | |
|---|---|---|
| Criminal Justice 101 | Introduction to Criminal Justice | 3 credits |
| Law 203 | Constitutional Law | 3 credits |

| | | |
|---|---|---|
| Sociology 203 | Criminology | 3 credits |
| Corrections 201 | The Law and Institutional Treatment | 3 credits |
| Law 206 | The American Judiciary | 3 credits |
| Police Science 201 | Police Organization and Administration | 3 credits |
| Statistics 250 | Principles and Methods of Statistics | 3 credits |
| Literature 327 | Crime and Punishment in Literature | 3 credits |
| Philosophy 321 | Police Ethics | 3 credits |
| Police Science 245 | Seminar in Community Policing | 3 credits |
| Police Science 401 | Seminar in Police Problems | 3 credits |

For an associate's (two-year) degree, majoring in criminal justice, you would take courses such as:

| | | |
|---|---|---|
| CRIJ 1301 | Introduction to Criminal Justice | 3 credits |
| CRIJ 1306 | Courts and Criminal Procedure | 3 credits |
| CRIJ 1307 | Crime in America | 3 credits |
| CRIJ 1310 | Fundamentals of Criminal Law | 3 credits |
| CJCR 1307 | Correctional Systems and Practices | 3 credits |
| CJSA 2300 | Legal Aspects of Law Enforcement | 3 credits |

For an associate's (two-year) degree, majoring in criminology, your core course work could include:

| | | |
|---|---|---|
| CRIM 150 | Introduction to the Criminal Justice System | 3 credits |
| CRIM 200 | Criminology | 3 credits |
| CRIM 201 | Institutional and Commercial Security | 3 credits |
| CRIM 210 | Introduction to Corrections | 3 credits |
| CRIM 220 | Introduction to Law Enforcement | 3 credits |
| CRIM 280 | The Law of Criminal Justice | 3 credits |
| CRIM 285 | Introduction to Criminalistics | 3 credits |
| CRIM 298 | Practicum in Criminal Justice | 3 credits |

For all degrees, you will probably be required to take the remainder of your credits in courses such as sociology, math, accounting, computers, writing/composition, psychology, government, and philosophy.

## CHOOSING A SCHOOL

Selecting the college or university that will best suit your needs, likes, and goals means making many decisions, including those about the type of school (community college, two- or four-year institution), overall size of the school, location, and quality of programs. Would you prefer a single-sex or co-ed environment? Large classes held in lecture halls, or smaller classes in which you get to know your professors? Do you want to go a local school and live at home, or are you willing to relocate and perhaps live in on-campus housing?

You can explore these options and many others by enlisting the help of an experienced high-school guidance counselor or career counselor. Keep asking questions—of yourself and them—until you have the information you need to make your decision. If you are not currently in school, use the guidebooks listed below, and the resources listed in the appendix at the end of this book, to help you. And whether you are in school or not, you should talk with those who are already working in law enforcement about their experiences. Ask where they went to school, what advantages they gained from their education, and what they would do differently if they were starting again.

Keep in mind during your search that there are three types of schools offering college credit. If you are interested in a two-year degree, will live at home, and work while getting your education, you might consider a community college. These are public institutions offering vocational and academic courses both during the day and at night. They typically cost less than both two- and four-year public and private institutions. You will need a high school diploma or GED to get in, and, depending on your course of study, you could have one of the following when you are finished:

- a certificate
- a license
- an AA degree (associate of arts)
- an AS degree (associate of science)
- an AAS degree (associate of applied science)

You can find out the location of community colleges in your area by contacting your state's Department of Education. Or check the world wide web through a search engine such as Yahoo.com for community colleges, which are listed by state.

## JUST THE FACTS

Still in high school? You may be able to receive some college credits by enrolling as a "guest student" or auditor at your local community college. Get a copy of the school's course list, and pick out one or two you are interested in. Then contact the admissions director. Explain your career plans and interest in sitting in on a course. You'll have to pay for it, but in many cases the credit is transferable when you enter college for a degree.

Junior colleges are two-year institutions that are usually more expensive than community colleges because they tend to be privately owned. You can earn a two-year degree (AA or AS), which can usually be applied to four-year programs at most colleges and universities. Use the Internet or the best-selling guide *Peterson's Two-Year Colleges* to help you with your search.

Colleges and universities offer undergraduate (usually four-year) programs in which you can earn a bachelor's (and often master's and doctoral) degree in a variety of fields. Entrance requirements are more stringent than for community colleges; admissions personnel will expect you to have taken certain classes in high school to meet their admission standards. Your high school GPA (grade point average) and standardized test scores (most often the Scholastic Aptitude Test or SAT) will be considered. If your high school grades are weak or if it has been some time since you were last in school, you might want to consider taking courses at a community college to bring you up to speed. You can always apply to the college or university as a transfer student after your academic track record has improved.

Be aware that state or public colleges and universities are less expensive to attend than private colleges and universities because they receive state funds to offset their operational costs. Another thing to consider when choosing a college is their placement programs in law enforcement. Do they have a relationship with area law enforcement agencies, in which the agencies actively recruit on campus, and may even use the campus as the site for their law enforcement academies? Attending a school with such a relationship could greatly improve your chances of employment upon graduation.

## Online College Guides

Most of these sites offer similar information, including various search methods, the ability to apply to many schools online, financial aid and scholarship information, and online test-taking (PSAT, SAT, etc.). Some offer advice in selecting schools, give virtual campus tours, and help you decide what classes to take in high school. It is well worth it to visit several of them.

www.embark.com—a good general site

www.collegequest.com—run by Peterson's, a well-known publisher of college guide books (they can also be found at www.petersons.com)

www.review.com—a service of *The Princeton Review*. Plenty of "insider information" on schools, custom searches for school, pointers on improving standardized test scores

www.collegenet.com—on the web since 1995, best for applying to schools online

www.collegereview.com—offers good general information, plus virtual campus tours

www.theadmissionsoffice.com—answers your questions about the application process, how to improve your chances of getting accepted, when to take tests

## College Guidebooks

### The Fiske Guide to Colleges 2000

*Edward B. Fiske, with Robert Logue. Crown Publishing Group, 1999.*

Fiske is the former education editor of the *New York Times*. His guide focuses on the "best and most interesting" 300+ colleges and universities. They are selected on the basis of their academic strength. Also included is a list of "best buys."

### Barron's Profiles of American Colleges, with Windows and Mac software

*College Division of Barron's Educational Series, 1998.*

This book rates every accredited four-year college and university in the United States. It includes an index of majors, so you can zero in on those schools offering the program you want, plus software that guides you through the preparation of admission forms and letters.

**The Insider's Guide to the Colleges**

*The Staff of the Yale Daily News. St. Martin's Press, Inc., 1999.*

The most frank of the guides, and the only one researched and written by current college students. There are no statistics, course descriptions, or other "dry" information. What you will find is student-to-student advice on the admissions process, how to choose a school, and how to pay for your education, and portraits of the schools that cover many aspects of life on campus, including the condition of the dorms and the dating scene.

## FINDING MONEY FOR YOUR EDUCATION

Once you have decided where you want to go to school, and know how much it will cost, you can begin to figure out how you are going to pay for your education. The U.S. Department of Education, in their helpful publication *The Study Guide*, cites the results of a recent Gallup poll surveying 13- to 21-year-olds about the average cost of public education in two- and four-year colleges. It turns out that the people who were surveyed guessed the costs to be three times higher than they actually are. Their estimates for four-year private colleges weren't much better—they guessed the costs to be one-third higher than they are in reality.

That's not to say that a college education is cheap; some colleges can be very expensive. But even those institutions aren't necessarily out of reach if you are willing to look into financial aid prospects. There are many opportunities out there for funding; most fall into one of three categories:

1. Scholarships and Grants—this money is awarded to students for a wide variety of reasons, including good grades, financial need, future career plans, ancestry, and even hobbies.
2. Loans—you can get loans that are backed by state and federal dollars to finance your education. Unlike grants and scholarships, they must be paid back with interest. However, interest rates on student loans are usually lower than any other kind of loan.

3. Work Study—this can be done either while in school (your school finds the job, you do the work, and you get the paycheck) or already working (your employer pays you back the money you spend on your education).

## Expenses to Expect

The two most expensive elements of a college education are tuition and room and board. Tuition is what you are charged for your classes. It can range from a few hundred dollars a year at a community college to tens of thousands of dollars at a private four-year school. Room and board is what you will pay to live in student housing and eat your meals at the school's dining halls. This cost can be greatly reduced (or even eliminated) if you live at home while in school.

For example, John Jay College of Criminal Justice, a liberal arts college within the City University of New York system, charges in-state residents $1,600 per semester in tuition if they are full-time students taking 12 or more credit hours. Tuition for part-time, in-state residents is $135 per credit hour. Foreign students and out-of-state residents can expect to pay $3,275 per semester if they attend full-time. Fees for a full-time student (12 or more credit hours) at John Jay are $50.75 per semester. A part-time student (less than 12 credit hours) pays $41.00 per semester.

As mentioned earlier, community colleges are usually the least expensive choices for education once you leave high school. The U.S. Department of Education found that most community colleges charge under $1,500 per year on average for tuition and fees. They also found plenty of four-year colleges and universities (public institutions, not private) that charge less than $3,000 per year in tuition and fees.

On the higher end of the spectrum, the County College of Morris, in Randolph, New Jersey, charges their full-time students $67 per credit if the student lives in the college's county. Out-of-county students can expect to pay $144 per credit. Even with fees, an associate's degree for an in-county student will cost under $5,000.

Tuition and fees aren't the only costs to consider, of course. Other costs for attending college include:

- books and supplies
- room and board
- transportation costs
- miscellaneous expenses

## Scholarships and Grants

Money for scholarships and grants is available for just about every student. Anything from being in the top 10% of your high school graduating class, to being an African American or a woman interested in a law enforcement career, to playing the piano could make you eligible. And while they probably won't be the sole means of financing your college education (most range from a few hundred to a few thousand dollars a year), scholarships and grants shouldn't be overlooked as a source of financing. Be sure to report them to the financial aid office of the college you attend.

One scholarship that considers ancestry is awarded by The National Organization of Black Law Enforcement Executives (NOBLE). A $1,000 scholarship is given to a high school senior, male or female, who is African American, has a minimum GPA of 2.5 and is planning to study criminal justice, law, or a related field. Financial need is a consideration. NOBLE's various chapters throughout the country offer about 35 similar scholarships. For further information, write to:

Noble National Office
4609 Pinecrest Office Park Drive, Suite F
Alexandria, VA 22312-1442
(703) 658-1529

Women going into a career in Law Enforcement might apply for a scholarship with the National Association of Law Enforcement Executives (www.nawlee.com), while those with a sports background could contact the NCAA at (913) 339-1906 to find out about scholarships and other funding for athletes.

However, the best way to find scholarship and grant money is to use one of the free search tools available on the Internet. You enter the appropriate information about yourself, and a search will take place which will give you a list of those prizes for which you are eligible. Try www.fastasp.org, which bills itself as the world's largest and oldest private sector scholarship database. Other good sites for conducting searches are www.college-scholarships.com and www.gripvision.com. If you don't have easy access to the Internet or want to expand your search, your high school guidance counselors or college financial aid officers also have plenty of information about available scholarship and grant money. It's wise to be cautious of sites or organizations that *guarantee* you money; check anything that sounds too good to be true with your college's financial aid office. While most scholarship search firms or databases are perfectly legitimate, there have been scams reported, so it pays to be aware.

### JUST THE FACTS

As a student, you can join the American Criminal Justice Association, as well as some other professional organizations. The ACJA awards scholarships and other awards and holds an annual student essay competition. They also hold job fairs at their national conferences. Reach them at acjalae.org. Look for other organizations online using the keywords "law enforcement organization."

## Loans

Although scholarships and grants, and even work-study programs, can help to offset the costs of higher education, they usually don't give you enough money to pay your way entirely. Most students who can't afford to pay for their entire education rely at least in part on student loans. The largest single source of these loans, and for all money for students, is the federal government. Try these three sites for information about the United States government's programs:

| | |
|---|---|
| www.fedmoney.org | This site explains everything from the application process (you can actually download the applications you'll need), eligibility requirements and the different types of loans available. |
| www.finaid.org | Here, you can find a calculator for figuring out how much money your education will cost (and |

how much you'll need to borrow), get instructions for filling out the necessary forms, and even find information on the various types of military aid (which will be detailed in the next chapter).

www.ed.gov/offices/OSFAP/students — The Federal Student Financial Aid Homepage. The FAFSA (Free Application for Federal Student Aid) can be filled out and submitted online.

You can also get excellent detailed information about different sources of federal education funding by sending away for a copy of the U.S. Department of Education's publication, *The Student Guide*. Write to:

Federal Student Aid Information Center
P.O. Box 84
Washington, DC 20044
1-800-4FED-AID

Loan money is also available from state governments. Below is a list of the agencies responsible for giving out such loans.

**ALABAMA**

Alabama Commission on Higher Education
100 North Union Street
P.O. Box 302000
Montgomery, AL 36130-2000
(334) 242-2276

**ALASKA**

Alaska Commission on Postsecondary Education
3030 Vintage Boulevard
Juneau, AK 99801-7109
(907) 465-6741
Fax: (907) 465-5316

**ARIZONA**

Arizona Commission for Postsecondary Education
2020 North Central Avenue, Suite 275
Phoenix, AZ 85004-4503
(602) 229-2591
Fax: (602) 229-2599
Web Address: www.acpe.asu.edu

**ARKANSAS**

Arkansas Department of Education
4 State Capitol Mall, Room 107A
Little Rock, AR 72201-1071
(501) 682-4396
E-mail Address: finaid@adhe.arknet.edu

### CALIFORNIA

California Student Aid Commission
P.O. Box 419026
Rancho Cordova, CA 95741-9026
Customer Service Department: (916) 526-7590
Fax: (916) 323-2619

### COLORADO

Colorado Commission on Higher Education
Colorado Heritage Center
1300 Broadway, 2nd Floor
Denver, CO 80203
(303) 866-2723
Fax: (303) 860-9750

### CONNECTICUT

Connecticut Department of Higher Education
61 Woodland Street
Hartford, CT 06105-2326
(860) 947-1855
Fax: (860) 947-1311

### DELAWARE

Delaware Higher Education Commission
Carvel State Office Building, 4th Floor
820 North French Street
Wilmington, DE 19801
(302) 577-3240
Fax: (302) 577-6765

### DISTRICT OF COLUMBIA

Department of Human Services
Office of Postsecondary Education Research and Assistance
2100 Martin Luther King Jr. Avenue SE, Suite 401
Washington, DC 20020
(202) 727-3688
Fax: (202) 727-2739

### FLORIDA

Florida Department of Education
Office of Student Financial Assistance
1344 Florida Education Center
325 West Gaines Street
Tallahassee, FL 32399-0400
(888) 827-2004
Fax: (850) 488-3612

### GEORGIA

Georgia Student Finance Commission
2082 East Exchange Place, Suite 100
Tucker, GA 30084
(770) 724-9030
Web Address: www.gsfc.org

### HAWAII

Hawaii State Postsecondary Education Commission
2444 Dole Street, Room 209
Honolulu, HI 96822-2394
(808) 956-8207
Fax: (808) 956-5156

### IDAHO

Idaho State Board of Education
P.O. Box 83720
Boise, ID 83720-0037
(208) 334-2270
Fax: (208) 334-2632

**ILLINOIS**

Illinois Student Assistance Commission (ISAC)
1755 Lake Cook Road
Deerfield, IL 60015-5209
(800) 899-4722
Web Address: www.isac-online.org

**INDIANA**

State Student Assistance Commission of Indiana
150 West Market Street, Suite 500
Indianapolis, IN 46204-2811
(317) 232-2350
Fax: (317) 232-3260

**IOWA**

Iowa College Student Aid Commission
200 10th St., 4th Floor
Des Moines, IA 50309-3609
(515) 281-3501
E-mail Address: csac@max.state.ia.us
Web Address: www.iowacollegeaid.org

**KANSAS**

Kansas Board of Regents
700 S.W. Harrison, Suite 1410
Topeka, KS 66603-3760
(785) 296-3517
Fax: (785) 296-0983
E-mail Address: christy@kbor.state.ks.us
Web Address: www.ukans.edu/~kbor

**KENTUCKY**

Kentucky Higher Education Assistance Authority (KHEAA)
1050 U.S. 127 South
Frankfort, KY 40601-4323
(800) 928-8926
Fax: (502) 696-7345
E-mail Address: Webmaster@kheaa.com
Web Address: www.kheaa.com

**LOUISIANA**

Louisiana Office of Student Financial Assistance
P.O. Box 91202
Baton Rouge, LA 70821-9202
(800) 259-5626 ext. 1012
(225) 922-1012
Fax: (225) 922-1089
E-mail Address for students: custserv@osfa.state.la.us or
webmaster@osfa.state.la.us
Web Address: www.osfa.state.la.us

**MAINE**

Finance Authority of Maine
P.O. Box 949
Augusta, ME 04332-0949
(800) 228-3734
(207) 623-3263
Fax: (207) 626-8208
TDD: (207) 626-2717
E-mail Address: info@famemaine.com

**MARYLAND**

Maryland Higher Education Commission
Jeffrey Building, 16 Francis Street
Annapolis, MD 21401-1781
(410) 974-5370
Fax: (410) 974-5994

**MASSACHUSETTS**

Massachusetts Board of Higher Education
Office of Student Financial Assistance
330 Stuart Street, 3rd Floor
Boston, MA 02116
(617) 727-1205
Fax: (617) 727-0667

**MICHIGAN**

Michigan Higher Education Assistance Authority
Office of Scholarships and Grants
P.O. Box 30462
Lansing, MI 48909-7962
(517) 373-3394
Fax: (517) 335-5984

**MINNESOTA**

Minnesota Higher Education Services Office
1450 Energy Park Drive, Suite 350
St. Paul, MN 55108-5227
(800) 657-3866
(651) 642-0567
Web Address: www.mheso.state.mn.us

**MISSISSIPPI**

Mississippi Postsecondary Education
Financial Assistance Board
3825 Ridgewood Road
Jackson, MS 39211-6453
(601) 982-6663
Fax: (601) 982-6527

**MISSOURI**

Missouri Student Assistance Resource Services (MOSTARS)
3515 Amazonas Drive
Jefferson City, MO 65109-5717
(800) 473-6757
(573) 751-3940
Fax: (573) 751-6635
Web Address: www.mocbhe.gov/mostars/finmenu.htm

**MONTANA**

Office of Commissioner of Higher Education
Montana Guaranteed Student Loan Program
P.O. Box 203101
Helena, MT 59620-3101
(800) 537-7508
E-mail Address: scholars@mgslp.state.mt.us
Web Address: www.mgslp.state.mt.us

**NEBRASKA**

Coordinating Commission for Postsecondary Education
P.O. Box 95005
Lincoln, NE 68509-5005
(402) 471-2847
Fax: (402) 471-2886
Web Address: www.nol.org/NEpostsecondaryed

**NEVADA**

Nevada Department of Education
700 East Fifth Street
Carson City, NV 89701-5096
(775) 687-9200
Fax: (775) 687-9101

**NEW HAMPSHIRE**

Postsecondary Education Commission
2 Industrial Park Drive
Concord, NH 03301-8512
(603) 271-2555
Fax: (603) 271-2696
E-mail Address: jknapp@nhsa.state.nh.us
Web Address: www.state.nh.us

**NEW JERSEY**

Higher Education Student Assistance Authority
P.O. Box 540
Trenton, NJ 08625
(800) 792-8670
Fax: (609) 588-3316
Web Address: www.state.nj.us/treasury/osa

**NEW MEXICO**

New Mexico Commission on Higher Education
1068 Cerrillos Road
Santa Fe, NM 87501
(800) 279-9777
E-mail Address: highered@che.state.nm.us
Web Address: www.nmche.org

**NEW YORK**

New York State Higher Education Services Corporation
One Commerce Plaza
Albany, NY 12255
(888) 697-4372
Fax: (518) 473-3749

**NORTH CAROLINA**

North Carolina State Education Assistance Authority
P.O. Box 13663
Research Triangle Park, NC 27709-3663
(800) 700-1775
E-mail Address: information@ncseaa.edu

**NORTH DAKOTA**

North Dakota University System
North Dakota Student Financial Assistance Program
600 East Boulevard Avenue, Dept. 215
Bismarck, ND 58505-0230
(701) 328-4114
Fax: (701) 328-2961

**OHIO**

Ohio Board of Regents
P.O. Box 182452
Columbus, OH 43218-2452
(888) 833-1133
Fax: (614) 752-5903

**OKLAHOMA**

Oklahoma State Regents for Higher Education
500 Education Building
Oklahoma City, OK 73105-4503
(405) 858-4356
Fax: (405) 858-4577

**OREGON**

Oregon State Scholarship Commission
1500 Valley River Drive, Suite 100
Eugene, OR 97401-2130
(800) 452-8807
Fax: (541) 687-7419
Web Address: www.ossc.state.or.us

**PENNSYLVANIA**

Pennsylvania Higher Education Assistance Authority
1200 North Seventh Street
Harrisburg, PA 17102-1444
(800) 692-7435
Web Address: www.pheaa.org

**RHODE ISLAND**

Rhode Island Higher Education Assistance Authority
560 Jefferson Boulevard
Warwick, RI 02886
(401) 736-1170
Fax: (401) 736-3541
TDD: (401) 222-6195

**SOUTH CAROLINA**

South Carolina Higher Education Tuition Grants Commission
P.O. Box 12159
Columbia, SC 29211
(803) 734-1200
Fax: (803) 734-1426
Web Address: www.state.sc.us/tuitiongrants

**SOUTH DAKOTA**

Department of Education and Cultural Affairs
Office of the Secretary
700 Governors Drive
Pierre, SD 57501-2291
(605) 773-3134
Fax: (605) 773-6139

**TENNESSEE**

Tennessee Student Assistance Corporation
404 James Robertson Parkway, Suite 1950
Nashville, TN 37243
(800) 342-1663
(615) 741-1346
Fax: (615) 741-6101
Web Address: www.state.tn.us/tsac

**TEXAS**

Texas Higher Education Coordinating Board
P.O. Box 12788, Capitol Station
Austin, TX 78711
(800) 242-3062
Fax: (512) 427-6420

**UTAH**

Utah State Board of Regents
Utah System of Higher Education
355 West North Temple
#3 Triad Center, Suite 550
Salt Lake City, UT 84180-1205
(801) 321-7200
Fax: (801) 321-7299

**VERMONT**

Vermont Student Assistance Corporation
P.O. Box 2000
Winooski, VT 05404-2601
(800) 642-3177
(800) 655-9602
Fax: (800) 654-3765
E-mail Address: info@vsac.org
Web Address: www.vsac.org

**VIRGINIA**

State Council of Higher Education for Virginia
James Monroe Building
101 North Fourteenth Street
Richmond, VA 23219-3684
(804) 786-1690
Fax: (804) 225-2604

**WASHINGTON**

Washington State Higher Education Coordinating Board
P.O. Box 43430
917 Lakeridge Way
Olympia, WA 98501-3430
(360) 753-7850
Fax: (360) 753-7808
E-mail Address: info@hecb.wa.gov
Web Address: www.hecb.wa.gov

**WEST VIRGINIA**

State College & University Systems of West Virginia Central Office
1018 Kanawha Boulevard East, Suite 700
Charleston, WV 25301-2827
(304) 558-4016
Fax: (304) 558-0259

**WISCONSIN**

Higher Educational Aids Board
P.O. Box 7885
Madison, WI 53707-7885
(608) 267-2944
Fax: (608) 267-2808
Web Address: http://heab.state.wi.us

**WYOMING**

Wyoming Community College Commission
2020 Carey Avenue, 8th Floor
Cheyenne, WY 82002
(307) 777-7763
Fax: (307) 777-6567

## WORK-STUDY OPTIONS

When applying to a college or university, you can indicate that you are interested in a work-study program. You'll then be given the details about the types of jobs offered under various programs (they can range from giving tours of the campus to prospective students to working in the cafeteria), any restrictions on employment, and how much they pay.

There is also the possibility of getting money for college by first securing a job in law enforcement with an agency that agrees to pay all or part of your educational expenses. Many departments offer a tuition reimbursement program. The amount of reimbursement is often tied to what kind of grades you make. The San Antonio Police Department, for example, pays 100% of your tuition if you make an "A," 75% for a "B," and 50% for a "C." Some departments will only pay for classes related to your job. "Job-related" may be defined in a detailed formal policy, or you may have to get your classes approved on a case-by-case basis.

Some departments make it even easier to attend college by permitting supervisors to adjust your work shifts and schedules so that you can attend classes. Other agencies offer scholarships or other financial incentives not only for college classes, but also for advanced state certification courses and certain in-service training programs.

### Police Corps

Another type of work-study arrangement is the Police Corps. If you agree to work in a state or local police force for a minimum of four years, the Police Corps program, run by the U.S. Department of Justice, will contribute funds to cover the following expenses:

- tuition
- fees
- books
- supplies

- transportation
- room and board

They have money for miscellaneous costs as well. You can receive up to $7,500 per academic year, for a total of up to $30,000. This program is designed primarily for college students who do not have prior policing experience. You must be in school full-time, pursuing a four-year degree, in order to apply. In addition to having good grades, you should be prepared to be evaluated for your physical and moral aptitude as well. The Corps looks for candidates who meet their standards and who will be committed to the goals of the program, which are as follows:

- to reduce crime and the fear of crime by adding college-educated officers trained in the principles of community-oriented patrol
- to choose candidates from a diverse population who are intelligent, well-educated, and highly qualified physically and morally
- to offer training experiences that stress professional competence and offer the opportunity to establish positive links between police and citizens. Police officers will have an understanding and empathy for those living in the area they patrol
- to provide a course of study that involves problem-solving, critical analysis and technological applications combined with an appreciation of community values and personal integrity

The Police Corps is run by individual state programs, and it is to those programs that you need to apply. For information, visit the Office of the Police Corps and Law Enforcement Education Web site at www.ojp.usdoj.gov/opclee. You can also call the U.S. Department of Justice Response Center at 1-800-421-6770 for specifics, including a detailed listing of participating states and points of contact.

After graduation, you will attend a training program for approximately 12 weeks. You will receive a salary at this point. Once training is completed, you will begin work. What's in it for the police department who agrees to hire you? They'll get $10,000 for each year of required service that you complete.

## INTERNSHIPS

An internship is one way to get job experience before you enter the "real" workforce. Although there are basically three types of internships, they are all designed as learning experiences, giving the intern exposure to an actual working environment. Internships can be one of the following:

- paid—the intern receives a salary for his/her work.
- college—the intern is a student, and usually receives college credit for his/her work.
- summer—the intern is likely to be a student, who may or may not receive college credit.

There are an almost limitless number of internships in criminal justice, law enforcement, and corrections. If you are already in school, your career placement office may have information regarding internships that have already been held by other students. Your school may have a relationship with local law enforcement agencies that can benefit you. Many colleges hire police officers to teach criminal justice courses; if you take these courses, you will be making contacts that can lead to an internship.

A sample of internship placements for the students in an undergraduate criminal justice program includes those at:

Police departments
Sheriffs departments
Adult courts
Juvenile programs
Forensics Labs
U.S. Secret Service
Corrections departments
FBI (summer internships)

To find contact persons for these types of internships, do some investigating on the Internet. Two sites which may be helpful are www.internships.com, which includes searches by region of the country and housing guides, if you are thinking of taking an internship in another area of the country, and www.internjobs.com, which has extensive listings of internships in police departments and the federal government.

It is also possible to create your own internship. You can approach the department or agency you'd like to intern for and ask to be considered. Once you find a contact person, write him or her a cover letter. This could be a great opportunity for the department to receive some extra (unpaid) help, and for you to receive invaluable experience.

Having an internship on your resume will make you stand out to a recruiter for a number of reasons:

1. You are already familiar with a professional environment and know what is expected of you.
2. You have proven yourself through performance to a potential employer.
3. After evaluating the realities of the job, you are still eager to pursue it.

It is also possible to make such a good impression during your internship that you are asked to apply for a full-time position. For all of these reasons, it can make great sense for you to get an internship.

## THE INSIDE TRACK

**Who:** Dr. Penny Shtull
**What:** Professor, Criminal Justice Dept.
**Where:** Norwich University, Northfield, Vermont
**How long:** Six years
**Degree:** Ph.D. in Criminal Justice, M.Phil. and M.A. in Forensic Psychology, from John Jay College of Criminal Justice, New York City; Bachelor's degree in Social Work from McGill University, Montreal

When I was in college and graduate school, I had the opportunity to do a number of internships. They let me get an inside view of law enforcement and helped me to decide what kind of career I wanted. The internships I took had me working in a forensic psychiatry clinic, a youth center, a hospital forensic unit, and various correctional facilities. I was able to explore my interests, gain experience in the field, get my foot in the door, and make contacts.

In the field of Criminal Justice, the trend is for increased education. Going to college will give you, as it gave me, an opportunity to explore the profession before you're actually in it. You will learn about the history and nature of the criminal justice field, gain an understanding of how the court, policing, and correctional systems work, go on ride-alongs with police officers, and study the nature and extent of crime. Although it is a traditionally male-dominated profession, the number of women is increasing, and I would encourage women to pursue a career in the field.

My students have diverse interests, including future work as police officers, attorneys, and caseworkers in correctional facilities. Studying criminal justice can help all of them prepare for their futures. While in school, they can continue to explore career choices, and get real experience. I encourage them to do internships or volunteer to get an insider's perspective.

Even as a professor, I continue to be actively involved in this dynamic field through volunteer work on boards such as the Department of Corrections' Community Reparative Probation Board and a Correctional Educational Advisory Board. There are also opportunities to participate in many professional organizations. My advice to those looking to get into a career in law enforcement is to get involved as soon as you can, and once you're working in the field, stay involved.

# CHAPTER three

## BECOMING A CANDIDATE: THE MILITARY OPTION

THERE ARE many advantages to joining the military if you are planning a career in law enforcement. This chapter will detail these advantages, as well as explain the five branches that make up the military, the four routes to the military, and how military service can help to pay for your education. Armed with this information, and with leads to finding much more, you will be able to decide whether the military option is right for you, and if it is, how and in what way you should serve.

**TRADITIONALLY, THE** military has been a great way to start a career in law enforcement. You can start gaining job experience before the age of 21, and future employers may put you above other candidates who didn't serve their country. Be aware, however, that military service should not be looked at as an alternative to higher education. As detailed in the previous chapter, the national trend is moving toward requiring a college degree from law enforcement candidates. Michael Berkow, Chief of the South Pasadena, CA, Police Department, says:

> I think that the military is a good first step but no longer the crucial step it was. Getting a degree is becoming more important. In 1990, only four police departments required a BA before hiring; that number is now over 100 and growing.

For every route to the military explained in this chapter, the advantages for helping you to earn a degree will be explored. No matter how you serve, you will be able to combine service with education.

## ADVANTAGES

Most law enforcement agencies set a minimum age for employment at 21. If you are younger, and are serious about your pursuit of a career in law enforcement, consider that by the time you reach that age, it is expected that you will be more than just a legal adult. Recruiters look for applicants who are mature, have life experience, and have proven to be responsible. You will want to possess these qualities by the time you are able to apply for a job in law enforcement. Sergeant Julie O'Brien, a supervisor for the Austin Police Department and an Army veteran says:

> Lack of life experience is the hardest obstacle to overcome. I think it's harder to do the job when you don't have much life experience. What you are likely to see in law enforcement can be overwhelming enough if you already have life experience; it can be much harder to deal with if you are coming at the situation without it. You can get life experience in the military.

If you don't have the inclination or funding to attend college full time, and are not yet twenty-one, joining the military can be a successful path toward your career goals. Law enforcement recruiters will look favorably on your choice as excellent preparation for work in the field.

Another benefit to military service is veteran's preference points. Veterans of military service are generally given preference points by most law enforcement agencies at local, state, and federal levels. Congress enacted laws long ago to make sure that those who serve their country aren't denied civilian jobs after they are discharged from the service. This means that many agencies will automatically add points to the test scores of veterans who apply to their agencies. At the federal level, veterans can receive anywhere from five to ten preference points, depending on the circumstances surrounding their military careers.

President Clinton made hiring military veterans very attractive to police departments. As part of his strategy to put more cops on the street, he supported a federal grant that pays participating police departments $10,000 for every veteran they hire (as long as the veteran held a job in the military that meets certain requirements). Before departments are paid, however, that veteran has to pass all police officer training and licensing requirements.

Those are not the only advantages. Additionally, law enforcement managers seem to prefer having veterans in their ranks. Sergeant O'Brien explains:

> I like to have former military personnel on my shift because they know the system. The structures of police departments are always going to be paramilitary so prior military personnel have an advantage because they are familiar with rank structure. They also react well in tactical situations—they follow orders quickly and without question.

## THE FIVE BRANCHES OF THE MILITARY

Although there are many similarities to the branches of the military, there are also significant differences. Sorting out the information about each one, and making a final decision about the best branch for you, will require some investigative skills. Locally, you can consult your phonebook's yellow pages under "Recruiting." This will give you the phone numbers and addresses of the nearest military recruiting offices, or you can look in the government blue pages for each of the individual branches. At the federal level, the branches may be contacted by e-mail or telephone:

| | | |
|---|---|---|
| U.S. Army | www.goarmy.com | 1-800-USA-ARMY |
| U.S. Air Force | www.af.mil/ | 1-800-423-USAF |
| U.S. Navy | www.navy.mil/ | 1-800-USA-NAVY |
| U.S. Marines | www.usmc.mil/ | 1-800-MARINES |
| U.S. Coast Guard | www.uscg.mil/ | 1-800-GET-USCG |

The websites are very helpful. You can talk online with recruiters without giving your name, find out about enlistment bonuses, and even read about what to expect during basic training. By visiting each site, you can compare their tuition assistance programs, minimum length of service, and other details (for instance, the Coast Guard is the only branch of the military which opens all specialties, including combat, to women). There are also more general military sites, such as www.militaryinfo.com and www.defenselink.com, which can be good sources of information.

## FOUR ROUTES TO SERVICE

There are four different routes to serving your country in the military:

1. enlist
2. attend a military academy
3. get an ROTC scholarship
4. join the Reserves or National Guard

All these routes will give you the military experience that can help your future career in law enforcement, but there are advantages and disadvantages to each. If you enlist, you can spend as little as two years with the military, earn some college credits (often at no cost to you), and come away with money to complete your education and with the life and work experience recruiters look for. Military academies are highly competitive, and although you will get a four-year degree at their expense, you will also have a commission, meaning you will serve in the military for a specified period of time after graduation. This is also true of the Reserve Officers Training Corps (ROTC) programs, although you will have a choice of where to attend school. Joining the Reserves or National Guard is the fourth route, which offers some money to help pay for schooling, while requiring part-time service in the military branch of your choice.

## IN THE NEWS

**Like Something Out of the Movies**

The Coast Guard has recently begun Operation New Frontier to combat the war on drugs. Using helicopters and high-speed small boats armed with state-of-the-art, non-lethal weapons, they are catching drug smuggling vessels known as "go-fasts." The high-tech, high-speed squadron is based in Jacksonville, Florida.

## The Enlistment Route

### Basic Requirements

While there are some variations between branches of the service, there are certain general requirements you will have to meet in order to enlist. You must:

- be between 18 and 34 years of age (if 17, you must have a parent or guardian's permission)
- be a U.S. citizen (or resident alien, in the case of the Coast Guard)
- have a high school diploma or GED (college credit can sometimes be a substitute)
- be drug-free
- have a clean arrest record

### Necessary Documents

You must present certain documents to your recruiter when you first start the enlistment process, and at various other points along the way. Have the following documentation available:

- a birth certificate or other proof of citizenship (or resident alien status) and date of birth
- a valid social security card or two other pieces of social security identification
- a high school diploma or GED certificate
- a letter or transcript documenting your midterm graduation from high school, if applicable
- a college transcript, if applicable, showing credits earned

- a parental or guardian consent form if you are under 18 years old
- a doctor's letter if you have, or have a history of, special medical condition(s)
- a marriage certificate, if applicable
- divorce papers, if applicable

### Meeting with a Recruiter

You can request application documents and speak with recruiters online, but eventually you will meet in person with a recruiter. The outcome of this meeting is supposed to be a signed contract between you and the military, so it is of utmost importance that you ask questions and do not sign until you are sure you understand exactly what will be required of you. Tony Gifford, a military police officer in the Army, discovered that sometimes people aren't aware of what military assignments are truly like:

> People coming into the Army's military policy (MP) are not aware that you do not just do law enforcement. You spend a lot of time in foreign countries keeping the peace, or whatever the Army wants you to do. Also, a lot of time is spent in the field training for combat. I don't mind it, but I was not aware of that until I got into the Army.

Ask about the service and its benefits: salaries, enlistment bonuses, postings, and educational opportunities, including financial aid for college. (See the table on the next page for the basic salaries of various grades of enlisted personnel in all the service branches.) The recruiter will also ask about your: education, physical and mental health, goals, interests, hobbies, and life experience. You should mention your desire to be a law enforcement agent.

You will be given a brief test designed to give the recruiter an idea of how well you will perform on the Armed Services Vocational Aptitude Battery (ASVAB). This pre-test covers math and vocabulary. Although the ASVAB has ten different subtests, it is the math and verbal portions that determine whether you pass. The other sections are designed to determine what your aptitudes are for different jobs. If everything has gone well up to this point, the recruiter will schedule you for a day at the Military Entrance Processing Station in your area (your travel expenses will be covered if you need to go a great distance, but there are stations in almost every state) for a day of written and physical testing.

## The 2000 Military Pay Chart

| Grade | Years of Service | | | | | | | | | | | | | |
|---|---|---|---|---|---|---|---|---|---|---|---|---|---|---|
| | <2 | 2 | 3 | 4 | 6 | 8 | 10 | 12 | 14 | 16 | 18 | 20 | 22 | 24 |
| **Commissioned Officers** | | | | | | | | | | | | | | |
| 0-10 | 8214.90 | 8503.80 | 8503.80 | 8503.80 | 8503.80 | 8830.20 | 8830.20 | 9319.50 | 9319.50 | 9986.40 | 9986.40 | 10655.10 | 10655.10 | 10655.10 |
| 0-9 | 7280.70 | 7471.50 | 7630.50 | 7630.50 | 7630.50 | 7824.60 | 7824.60 | 8150.10 | 8150.10 | 8830.20 | 8830.20 | 9319.50 | 9319.50 | 9319.50 |
| 0-8 | 6594.30 | 6792.30 | 6953.10 | 6953.10 | 6953.10 | 7471.50 | 7471.50 | 7824.60 | 7824.60 | 8150.10 | 8503.80 | 8830.20 | 9048.00 | 9048.00 |
| 0-7 | 5479.50 | 5851.80 | 5851.80 | 5851.80 | 6114.60 | 6114.60 | 6468.90 | 6468.90 | 6792.30 | 7471.50 | 7985.40 | 7985.40 | 7985.40 | 7985.40 |
| 0-6 | 4061.10 | 4461.60 | 4754.40 | 4754.40 | 4754.40 | 4754.40 | 4754.40 | 4754.40 | 4916.10 | 5693.10 | 5983.80 | 6114.60 | 6468.90 | 6687.30 |
| 0-5 | 3248.40 | 3813.90 | 4077.90 | 4077.90 | 4077.90 | 4077.90 | 4200.30 | 4427.10 | 4723.80 | 5077.50 | 5368.30 | 5531.10 | 5724.60 | 5724.60 |
| 0-4 | 2737.80 | 3333.90 | 3556.20 | 3556.20 | 3622.20 | 3781.80 | 4040.40 | 4267.50 | 4461.60 | 4658.10 | 4785.90 | 4785.90 | 4785.90 | 4785.90 |
| 0-3 | 2544.00 | 2844.30 | 3041.10 | 3364.80 | 3525.90 | 3652.20 | 3850.20 | 4040.40 | 4139.10 | 4139.10 | 4139.10 | 4139.10 | 4139.10 | 4139.10 |
| 0-2 | 2218.80 | 2423.10 | 2910.90 | 3009.00 | 3071.10 | 3071.10 | 3071.10 | 3071.10 | 3071.10 | 3071.10 | 3071.10 | 3071.10 | 3071.10 | 3071.10 |
| 0-1 | 1926.30 | 2004.90 | 2423.10 | 2423.10 | 2423.10 | 2423.10 | 2423.10 | 2423.10 | 2423.10 | 2423.10 | 2423.10 | 2423.10 | 2423.10 | 2423.10 |
| **Commissioned Officers with over 4 years active duty service as an enlisted member or warrant officer** | | | | | | | | | | | | | | |
| 0-3E | 0.00 | 0.00 | 0.00 | 3364.80 | 3525.90 | 3652.20 | 3850.20 | 4040.40 | 4200.30 | 4200.30 | 4200.30 | 4200.30 | 4200.30 | 4200.30 |
| 0-2E | 0.00 | 0.00 | 0.00 | 3009.00 | 3071.10 | 3168.60 | 3333.90 | 3461.40 | 3556.20 | 3556.20 | 3556.20 | 3556.20 | 3556.20 | 3556.20 |
| 0-1E | 0.00 | 0.00 | 0.00 | 2423.10 | 2588.40 | 2683.80 | 2781.30 | 2877.60 | 3009.00 | 3009.00 | 3009.00 | 3009.00 | 3009.00 | 3009.00 |
| **Warrant Officers** | | | | | | | | | | | | | | |
| W-5 | 0.00 | 0.00 | 0.00 | 0.00 | 0.00 | 0.00 | 0.00 | 0.00 | 0.00 | 0.00 | 0.00 | 4423.80 | 4591.20 | 4724.10 |
| W-4 | 2592.00 | 2781.30 | 2781.30 | 2844.30 | 2974.20 | 3105.00 | 3235.50 | 3461.40 | 3622.20 | 3749.40 | 3850.20 | 3874.10 | 4107.00 | 4235.10 |
| W-3 | 2355.90 | 2555.40 | 2555.40 | 2588.40 | 2618.70 | 2810.40 | 2974.20 | 3071.10 | 3168.60 | 3263.40 | 3364.80 | 3495.90 | 3622.20 | 3622.20 |
| W-2 | 2063.40 | 2232.60 | 2232.60 | 2297.40 | 2423.10 | 2555.40 | 2652.60 | 2749.80 | 2844.30 | 2944.50 | 3041.10 | 3136.80 | 3263.40 | 3263.40 |
| W-1 | 1719.00 | 1971.00 | 1971.00 | 2135.90 | 2232.60 | 2328.00 | 2423.10 | 2522.70 | 2618.70 | 2716.20 | 2810.40 | 2910.90 | 2910.90 | 2910.90 |

## The 2000 Military Pay Chart (Continued)

| Grade | Years of Service | | | | | | | | | | | | | |
|---|---|---|---|---|---|---|---|---|---|---|---|---|---|---|
| | <2 | 2 | 3 | 4 | 6 | 8 | 10 | 12 | 14 | 16 | 18 | 20 | 22 | 24 |
| **Enlisted Members** | | | | | | | | | | | | | | |
| **E-9** | 0.00 | 0.00 | 0.00 | 0.00 | 0.00 | 0.00 | 3015.30 | 3083.40 | 3152.70 | 3225.60 | 3298.20 | 3361.50 | 3537.90 | 3675.60 |
| **E-8** | 0.00 | 0.00 | 0.00 | 0.00 | 0.00 | 2528.40 | 2601.60 | 2669.70 | 2739.00 | 2811.60 | 2875.50 | 2946.30 | 3119.40 | 3258.00 |
| **E-7** | 1765.80 | 1906.20 | 1976.10 | 2045.70 | 2115.60 | 2182.80 | 2252.70 | 2323.20 | 2427.90 | 2496.90 | 2566.20 | 2599.50 | 2774.40 | 2912.40 |
| **E-6** | 1518.90 | 1655.70 | 1724.40 | 1797.50 | 1865.40 | 1932.60 | 2003.40 | 2106.60 | 2172.90 | 2242.80 | 2277.00 | 2277.00 | 2277.00 | 2277.00 |
| **E-5** | 1332.60 | 1450.50 | 1521.00 | 1587.30 | 1691.70 | 1761.00 | 1830.00 | 1898.10 | 1932.60 | 1932.60 | 1932.60 | 1932.60 | 1932.60 | 1932.60 |
| **E-4** | 1242.90 | 1312.80 | 1390.20 | 1497.30 | 1556.70 | 1556.70 | 1556.70 | 1556.70 | 1556.70 | 1556.70 | 1556.70 | 1556.70 | 1556.70 | 1556.70 |
| **E-3** | 1171.50 | 1235.70 | 1284.60 | 1335.90 | 1335.90 | 1335.90 | 1335.90 | 1335.90 | 1335.90 | 1335.90 | 1335.90 | 1335.90 | 1335.90 | 1335.90 |
| **E-2** | 1127.40 | 1127.40 | 1127.40 | 1127.40 | 1127.40 | 1127.40 | 1127.40 | 1127.40 | 1127.40 | 1127.40 | 1127.40 | 1127.40 | 1127.40 | 1127.40 |
| **E-1>4** | 1005.60 | 1005.60 | 1005.60 | 1005.60 | 1005.60 | 1005.60 | 1005.60 | 1005.60 | 1005.60 | 1005.60 | 1005.60 | 1005.60 | 1005.60 | 1005.60 |
| **E-1<4** | 930.30 | 0.00 | 0.00 | 0.00 | 0.00 | 0.00 | 0.00 | 0.00 | 0.00 | 0.00 | 0.00 | 0.00 | 0.00 | 0.00 |

### Key to Military Ranks

**Army Ranks:**
**E-1:** Recruit
**E-2:** Private
**E-3:** Private First Class
**E-4:** Corporal/Specialist
**E-5:** Sergeant
**E-6:** Staff Sergeant
**E-7:** Sergeant First Class
**E-8:** Master Sergeant
**E-9:** Sergeant Major

**Navy Ranks:**
**E-1:** Airman or Seaman or Fireman or Construction Recruit
**E-2:** Airman or Seaman or Fireman or Construction Apprentice
**E-3:** Airman or Seaman or Fireman or Construction
**E-4:** Petty Officer 3rd Class
**E-5:** Petty Officer 2nd Class
**E-6:** Petty Officer 1st Class
**E-7:** Chief Petty Officer
**E-8:** Senior Chief Petty Officer
**E-9:** Master Chief Petty Officer

**Air Force Ranks:**
**E-1:** Airman basic
**E-2:** Airman
**E-3:** Airman 1st Class
**E-4:** Senior Airman
**E-5:** Staff Sergeant
**E-6:** Technical Sergeant
**E-7:** Master Sergeant
**E-8:** Senior Master Sergeant
**E-9:** Chief Master Sergeant

**Marine Ranks:**
**E-1:** Private
**E-2:** Private First Class
**E-3:** Lance Corporal
**E-4:** Corporal
**E-5:** Sergeant
**E-6:** Staff Sergeant
**E-7:** Gunnery Sergeant
**E-8:** Either Master Sergeant or 1st Sergeant
**E-9:** Master Gunnery Sergeant or Sergeant Major

**Coast Guard Ranks:**
**E-1:** Recruit
**E-2:** Fireman or Seaman Apprentice
**E-3:** Fireman or Seaman
**E-4:** Petty Officer 3rd Class
**E-5:** Petty Officer 2nd Class
**E-6:** Petty Officer 1st Class
**E-7:** Chief Petty Officer
**E-8:** Senior Chief Petty Officer

## Enlistment by Branch

| Branch of Service | Terms of Enlistment |
|---|---|
| Army | 2, 4, or 6 years |
| Navy | 3, 4, 5, or 6 years |
| Air Force | 4 or 6 years |
| Marine Corps | 3, 4, or 5 years |

### Military Entrance Processing Station (MEPS)

The MEPS is where every applicant for each branch of the military begins the enlistment process. Schedules may vary a little from area to area, but they all operate five days per week and are open some Saturdays. If for any reason you are asked to stay overnight for testing, then the military will pay for your hotel room and meals. When you enter the MEPS, you will check in at the control desk, and then be sent to the liaison office for your chosen branch of service.

During your day at MEPS you will go through three phases:

- mental (aptitude) testing
- medical exam
- administrative procedures

Your schedule may vary somewhat from the one outlined here, depending on how much of the process you have completed in advance. Some applicants, for example, may have already taken the ASVAB at a Mobile Examining Team (MET) site near their hometown recruiting station.

### The ASVAB

Your day at the MEPS will begin with the ASVAB (unless you have already taken it). Because results of the ASVAB test are used to determine whether or not you can join the branch of the military you prefer, and which training programs you are qualified to enter, it makes sense to learn as much as you can about the test ahead of time. You can search the Internet for information and practice tests, and purchase study guides to improve your chances for a good score. (See LearningExpress' Armed Services Vocational Aptitude Battery [ASVAB] study guide or take a practice ASVAB online at www.learnatest.com.)

Some MEPS are now conducting ASVAB testing by computer. The computer version of the test takes one hour and 40 minutes to complete, as opposed to over three hours for the paper-and-pencil version. The computer ASVAB still consists of ten subtests, but it works differently than the paper version. The computer will display the first question, and, if you get this question right, it gives you another question on the same subject—but this question is harder than the first one. The questions get harder as you progress, and, after you answer a certain number correctly, the computer skips to the next subtest. For example, you could get eight questions right and then the computer might go to the next subtest instead of requiring you to answer all 25 questions in the first subtest.

Most MEPS do not have enough computers to test everyone. If you notice that some applicants are taken to a room with computer testing and the others are required to take the ASVAB with pen and paper, don't worry. Either way, the information and skills you need remain the same, and your evaluation will not be affected.

### Medical Exam

All the doctors you will see are civilians. You will see them at least three times during the day. During the first visit, you and the medical staff will thoroughly review your medical prescreening form, your medical history form, and all of the medical records you've been told by your recruiter to bring along. This meeting will be one-on-one.

After this meeting, you will move on to the examining room. You will strip down to your underwear and perform a series of about 20 exercises that will let the medical staff see how your limbs and joints work. You may be with a group of other applicants of the same sex during this examination, or you may be alone with the doctor.

During your third meeting with the doctor, you will receive a routine physical. Among the procedures you can expect are:

- blood pressure evaluation
- pulse rate evaluation
- heart and lung check
- evaluation of blood and urine samples
- eye exam
- hearing exam
- height-proportional-to-weight check
- chest X ray
- HIV testing

Female applicants will be given a pelvic/rectal examination. Another woman will be present during this procedure, but otherwise this exam will be conducted in private.

After the medical examinations are complete, you will be told your results. If the medical staff uncovers a problem that will keep you from joining the service, they will discuss the matter with you. In some cases the doctor may tell you that you are being disqualified now, but that you can come back at a later date to try again. For example, you can be disqualified if you are overweight; after dieting, you can come back to the MEPS for another try.

If the doctor wants to have a medical specialist examine you for some reason, you may have to stay overnight, or the doctor may schedule an appointment for a later date (at the military's expense). Unless you need to see a specialist, the medical exam should take no more than three hours.

### Paperwork

The rest of your day will be taken up with administrative concerns. First, you will meet with a guidance counselor for your branch of the service. He or she will take the results of your physical, your ASVAB scores, and all the other information you have provided and enter it into a computer system. The computer will show which military jobs you are best suited for. Then you can begin asking questions about your career options. The counselor will be able to tell you:

- which jobs you are qualified for
- which jobs suit your personality, abilities, and interests
- which jobs are available
- when the required training is available

### Delayed Entry Programs

Delayed entry programs allow you to enlist with your chosen branch of the military and report for duty up to 365 days later. This is a popular program for students who are still in high school or for those who have other obligations that prevent them from leaving for basic training right away. However, you should be aware that the seats in the popular training programs go fast. If it is possible for you to join immediately, you will increase your chances of getting the training you want.

### Basic Training

You will report back to the MEPS to prepare for Basic Training. If you have been in the Delayed Entry Program, you will get a last minute mini-physical to make sure your condition is still up to military standards. You will also be asked about any changes that might affect your eligibility since the last time you were at the MEPS, such as medical problems. If you have been arrested or had any medical problems, now is the time to speak up.

Your orders and records will be completed at the MEPS, and then you will be sent to Basic. Where you train will depend on the branch of service. The Air Force and Navy have only one training facility each. The Marines have two, and the Army has several, due to the many different specialized training paths they offer.

## Basic Training (by Branch)

| Branch | Location of Basic Training Facility | Length of Training |
|---|---|---|
| Army | Fort Benning, GA; Fort Knox, TN; Fort Sill, OK; Fort Bliss, TX; Fort Leonard Wood, MI; or Fort McClellan, AL | 8 weeks |
| Navy | Recruit Training Command, Great Lakes, IL | 8 weeks and 3 days |
| Air Force | Lackland Air Force Base, TX | 6 weeks |
| Marine Corps | Parris Island, SC; or San Diego, CA | Women: 12 weeks; Men: 11 weeks, plus 4 weeks of combat training |
| Coast Guard | Cape May, NJ | 8 weeks |

### The First Few Days

No matter which branch of service you join, the first few days of Basic are similar. You will spend time at an intake facility, where you will be assigned to a basic training unit and undergo a quick-paced introduction to your branch of service. Your days will include:

- orientation briefings
- uniform distribution

- records processing
- I.D. card preparation
- barracks upkeep training
- drill and ceremony instruction
- physical training (PT)

You will be assigned to a group of recruits ranging from 35 to 80 people. The Navy calls these training groups "companies," the Army and Marine Corps call them "platoons," and the Air Force calls them "flights." Your group will be led by a drill instructor. You will be supervised by this person from your early morning wake-up until you retire at night. He or she will be your primary instructor throughout basic training.

**JUST THE FACTS**

The Navy helps its sailors to get college degrees through its SMART program. The Sailor/Marine Corps American Council on Education Registry Transcript can be used during or after active duty when applying to colleges and universities nationwide. It lists college credit earned for military training and work experience. For instance, after going through boot camp, sailors have a transcript listing three college credits for physical education.

### The Following Weeks

From the intake facility, you move to your Basic Training site. The training day starts at around 5 A.M. and ends at around 9 P.M. Most Saturdays and Sundays are light training days. You will not have much free time, and your ability to travel away from your unit on weekends will be very limited, if you get this privilege at all. In most cases you will not be eligible to take leave (vacation time) until after Basic Training, although exceptions may be made in the case of a family emergency.

The subjects you will learn in Basic Training include:

- military courtesy
- military regulations
- military rules of conduct
- hygiene and sanitation

- organization and mission
- handling and care of weapons
- tactics and training related specifically to your service

While in Basic Training, you will receive plenty of physical training. Physical fitness is critical for trainees, and your drill instructor will keep tabs on your progress throughout Basic Training by giving you periodic tests. In order to do well through this training, it is advised that you start a running and weight-lifting program the instant you make your decision to join the military. Recruits in all branches of the service run mile after mile, perform hundreds of sit-ups and push-ups, and become closely acquainted with obstacle courses. These courses differ in appearance from facility to facility, but they all require the same things: plenty of upper body strength and overall endurance, as well as the will to succeed.

### Occupational Specialties

The military offers training in many areas that will be useful in a civilian law enforcement career. You do not necessarily need to choose the field of Military Police, according to Sergeant O'Brien:

> My first order of preference for people I want on my shift is prior military experience, regardless of the occupational skills they learned in the military.

All branches of the military basically offer the same career fields, although they are often called by different names. On the following page is a list of careers that could translate well to a law enforcement career. Further details may be obtained from a recruiter, though they should not vary greatly from branch to branch. The list below uses Army titles and Army requirements as examples.

**Requirements for Selected Military Occupational Specialties**

| Military Occupational Speciality | Physical Demands | Minimum ASVAB Composite Score | Other Requirements |
|---|---|---|---|
| Infantryman* | very heavy | CO 90 | red/green color discrimination, vision correctable to 20/20 in one eye and 20/100 in the other |
| PATRIOT Missile Crewmember | moderately heavy | OF 100 | red/green color discrimination, SECRET security clearance |
| Psychological Operations Specialist | medium | ST 105 | normal color vision, SECRET security clearance, minimum score on language test |
| Broadcast Journalist | light | GT 110 | ability to type 20 WPM, completion of at least two years of high school English, driver's license |
| Ammunition Specialist | very heavy | ST 100 | normal color vision, CONFIDENTIAL security clearance, not allergic to explosive components, not claustrophobic |
| Executive Administrative Assistant | not applicable | ST 105 | SECRET security clearance, ability to type 35 WPM, minimum score on English test |
| Legal Specialist | light | CL 110 | ability to type 35 WPM, no civil convictions |
| Finance Specialist | light | CL 95 | no record of dishonesty or moral turpitude |
| Watercraft Operator | very heavy | MM 100 | normal color vision, vision correctable to 20/20 in one eye and 20/40 in the other, prior training |
| Medical Specialist | moderately heavy | ST 95 | normal color vision |
| Behavioral Science Specialist | light | ST 105 | |
| Military Police | moderately heavy | ST 95 | red/green color discrimination, minimum height 5' 8" for males, 5' 4" for females, CONFIDENTIAL security clearance, driver's license, no record of civilian convictions |
| Intelligence Analyst | medium | ST 105 | normal color vision, TOP SECRET security clearance, no record, certain restrictions on foreign ties |

* Specialties not open to women.

Composite Score key: OF = Operations and Food Handling; ST = Skilled Technician; GT = General Technical; CL = Clerical; MM = Mechanical Maintenance; CO = Combat.

### College Education During Military Duty

As stressed in the previous chapter, a college education is of utmost importance to your future career, both in beating the competition to the job, and getting promoted and rewarded once you are in. Joining the military right out of high school does not mean that you cannot get a college education; it does not have to be an either-or choice. In fact, you can successfully combine the two, so that once you leave the military, you have enough college credits to apply for almost any job in law enforcement (see the following chapters for specific information regarding how much schooling is required for various jobs in law enforcement). Sergeant O'Brien says:

> If you join the military, there is no reason why you cannot get your education at the same time. It's a fact that you can communicate better if you are college-educated, and you will most likely need the college hours anyway. I think the military is a good source of life experience, but don't waste your time while you're in there. In a three-year stint you can easily get a two-year degree.

The military makes education programs available while you are on active duty or after you finish your military obligation. Your training and on-the-job experience can translate into college credits (for instance, basic training can earn three credits for physical education). Building on these credits, you can attend courses both in person and through the Internet while on active duty. Every branch of the service offers tuition assistance to help pay for these courses, and the Navy has even recently developed the Navy College Program (NCP) in order to encourage and aid sailors in the pursuit of college degrees during their Navy careers.

The other branches of the service are also making it easier to combine active duty with education. Air Force Senior Airman Julius Carl Mitchell earned his degree while on active duty. He is assigned to the Security Force (formerly the Security Police) and recently completed his associate degree in criminal justice through the Community College of the Air Force. Airman Mitchell says it would have been easier to attend his college classes had he gone into a specialty other than the Security Force, but he completed his degree nonetheless:

It all depended on where I was stationed at the time. While I was in Korea, it was easy. The problem is, law enforcement is a 24-hour organization. It's not hard if you are part of another organization in the Air Force, but since we don't necessarily work 9-to-5, it can be hard to get to class.

If you can't finish a degree during active service, the military offers help after your service ends. Some of the benefits include education loan repayments (up to $65,000 from the Army), enlistment bonuses to be used for tuition, and programs such as the Montgomery GI Bill (MGIB). As with all the information you get from a recruiter before you enlist, it is important to understand and get in writing exactly what these benefits are.

For instance, the MGIB is often used as an example of how the military will help you finance your education. What is sometimes not clear is how many limitations are placed on this money and how it can be used. Since 1984, the MGIB has been available to servicemen willing to contribute $100 per month for their first 12 months of service. This $1,200 is not refundable for any reason, and you will forfeit it completely if you receive anything less than an honorable discharge.

Once you leave the military, you have 10 years to use the education benefit. If you were enlisted three years or less, you will receive $347.65 per month to be used to get degrees, certificates, correspondence course credits, and vocational flight training. If you were enlisted for over three years, you will receive $427.87 per month. If you compare these amounts with the "expenses to expect" in Chapter 2, you will see that in most instances, the MGIB will not cover all your expenses.

Be aware, too, that most colleges and universities have financial aid personnel who are trained specifically to handle military education programs and benefits. Get advice and information from them, as well as from your local recruiter, and use one of the Internet search engines (like Yahoo! or Excite) to search the World Wide Web. Use the key words "Montgomery GI Bill" to find many informative articles (pro and con), charts, and detailed payment projection information.

## U.S. Military Academies

The decision to attend a military academy is one that requires great commitment, beginning in the first or second year of high school. You will need excellent grades and strong recommendations from your school and your state representative to get into one of these institutions. The competition for admission is fierce because of the prestige and quality of the education. And free tuition in return for your commitment to serve after graduation is certainly a selling point. "Prepare early" is the key phrase here. High school counselors have the information you need to formulate a strategy.

Except for the Marine Corps, each branch of the armed services has an academy. Upon graduation from their institution, you will receive a bachelor's degree and a commission in the military. The academies are:

- U.S. Military Academy, located in West Point, New York
- U.S. Naval Academy, located in Annapolis, Maryland
- U.S. Air Force Academy, located in Colorado Springs, Colorado

There are two other academy options: the U.S. Coast Guard Academy, located in New London, Connecticut, and the U.S. Merchant Marine Academy, located in Kings Point, New York. They offer the same incentives as the military academies in that they pay your tuition in return for your service in the Coast Guard or Merchant Marines.

## Reserve Officers Training Corps (ROTC) Programs

Another way to combine military service and higher education is to enroll in an ROTC program in college. The Navy, Marines, Army, and Air Force all offer ROTC, a college elective that you take along with your regular course work. The best way to take advantage of one of these programs is to apply for and get an ROTC scholarship. The military websites listed at the beginning of this chapter all have information about their ROTC programs, including lists of the hundreds of schools across the country that offer them. You can even fill out applications online.

Captain Rhonda Lovko, who is currently assigned to the Military Science Department at Santa Clara University in California, has this advice for high school seniors and recent graduates interested in ROTC:

> If you haven't gotten a scholarship by the time you are a senior in high school, it's too late for the first year of college. If you feel you are interested at all in ROTC, then go ahead and try it out for the first year or two. It's just a course, and if you don't like it you aren't under any obligation. You can apply for scholarships once you get past your freshman year.

ROTC scholarship programs will pay most of your tuition, fees, and textbook costs. They will also give you a monthly allowance while you are in school. In return, you commit to summer training while you are in school and to serve as an officer in that branch of the service after earning your bachelor's degree. This makes the ROTC programs similar to attendance at one of the academies: a free (or mostly free) education is followed by years of military service on your part. Captain Lovko sums it up:

> The hardest part for students to realize is that after you've been given money by the ROTC for your education, the services are going to want something back. You are going to have to go on active duty for at least four years after graduation in return for that money.

All of the ROTC branches have eligibility requirements for you to meet before they will give you an ROTC scholarship. The Army requires that:

- you must be a U.S. citizen at least 17 years old by October 1 and under 23 on June 30 of the year in which you are applying. You can't be older than 27 by June 30 of the year you'll graduate from college. If you have prior active-duty military service, you may get an extension of the age requirement: a one-year extension for every one year of prior service. However, they will only waive three years total.

- you must have a minimum SAT score of 920 points or an ACT composite score of 19.

The above-listed requirements are the primary ones, but the Army does have others for their ROTC scholarships.

A scholarship student can receive an additional $1,500 per year. Non-scholarship students can get that $1,500 per year if they sign as a contracted cadet with the Army in the last two years of school. After you get your degree and meet the commissioning requirements, you can fulfill your post-college commitment part-time in the National Guard or Reserve, or full-time in the active Army, earning approximately $26,000 per year in pay and allowances.

Air Force ROTC scholarships range in length from two to four years. The Air Force will pay full or partial tuition, give you an allowance for textbooks, and pay most of your fees. Once your scholarship begins, you will get an additional $150 per month to help with expenses. To be eligible, you must be under 27 years of age by June 30 of the year that you receive your commission, unless you are a prior service applicant. You also must pass the Air Force's Physical Fitness Test (PFT), which includes a 1.5 mile run, and then an Air Force medical exam. You must also pass the Air Force Officer Qualifying Test (AFOQT).

The Navy relies on their NROTC (Naval Reserve Officers' Training Corps) programs for the majority of their Navy and Marine Corps officers. Unlike the Army and Air Force programs, when the NROTC awards you a scholarship, they pay 100% of your tuition, books, and fees no matter where you go to school—public or private. (As in all the ROTC scholarship programs, you will pay your own room and board.) You will also get a $150 per month allowance during the school year. Plus, you will be paid for attending 30 days of active-duty training each summer. After graduation from an NROTC scholarship program, you will be a midshipman, commissioned as an officer in the unrestricted line of the Naval Reserve or Marine Corps Reserve.

Captain Lovko, who's also a 1991 graduate of Christopher Newport College's Army ROTC program, has a few thoughts to pass on to women who are interested in ROTC (advice that will also serve men):

I've never felt that this program was any more of a challenge simply because I am female. Don't let anybody tell you that you can't do it. It can be a little more challenging as far as physical fitness goes. You have to be in good enough shape to pass the physical testing and you have to meet height and weight requirements. It isn't that hard, but you have to do more than sit on the couch and watch TV to get ready.

## National Guard and Reserves

Enlisting full-time in the armed services might not be for everyone. The National Guard and Reserve programs offer a good alternative, especially if you are or plan to be in school full-time, and don't want to face more military service after graduation (as with the Academies or ROTC programs). After following the same procedures as for full-time enlistment (taking the ASVAB, passing a physical exam, etc.), you are on duty two weeks for annual training, and just one weekend a month for the rest of the year. You receive the same training (including Basic) and schooling as your active-duty counterparts. These programs can help with college costs through tuition reimbursement programs, and can also supplement your income while you go to school.

For information on the Army and Air National Guard programs, log onto the National Guard Bureau's website: www.ngb.dtic.mil/. Both programs are run by units—the Army has over 3,200 and the Air Force over 200. They are run with some differences from unit to unit, so it is important to contact a recruiter online or over the phone to get specifics. For instance, tuition assistance benefits range from the Army's offer of up to 75% for five classes per year (depending on your unit) to the Air Force's offer of up to 100% assistance.

The Army National Guard requires a minimum of three years of service, during which time you can not only stay in school (and get help paying for it), but receive Advanced Individual Training in one of dozens of Military Occupational Specialties (MOS). After training, you will be paid to work in your specialty (which might be military policing or surveillance). The Air

National Guard programs also vary from unit to unit. If you serve in Pennsylvania, for instance, you can enroll in the Community College of the Air Force and earn a two-year associate's degree in applied sciences. In addition, all of the training you receive as a member of the ANG is worth college credit.

The three branches of the Reserves are also run by state units. They continue to make changes to their programs to make enlistment more appealing. The benefits have been upgraded and new education incentives have been added. For more information, they may be contacted as follows:

| | | |
|---|---|---|
| U.S. Army Reserve | www.army.mil/usar/ | 1-800-USA-ARMY |
| U.S. Navy Reserve | www.navres.navy.mil/navresfor/ | 1-800-USA-USNR |
| U.S. Air Force Reserve | www.afreserve.com | 1-800-257-1212 |

## THE INSIDE TRACK

**Who:** Julius Carl Mitchell
**What:** Senior Airman
**Wher:** Randolph Air Force Base in San Antonio, Texas
**How long:** Over eight years in Air Force law enforcement
**Degree:** Six weeks of law enforcement academy; four weeks of air base defense; over a year of on-the-job training

I wanted to work in work in law enforcement. When I first got into the Air Force there were two different sides of house, so to speak—security and law enforcement. The security side guarded planes and things like that and on the law enforcement side you got to deal more with people—work investigations—things I wanted to do. I love meeting different kinds of people. I like being there to provide assistance for people that need it.

In a typical day, we have to come in an hour early for each shift. If we're scheduled to work eight-hour shifts, then you really end up putting in nine hours. If we're working 12-hour shifts, which we've been doing a lot lately because we have [personnel] shortages, then we actually put in 13 hours. My current duties are to check equipment in and out—weapons, mace, radios, and flashlights.

The first thing we do when we get to work is have Guard Mount, which is like roll call for civilan police officers. The day before you come into work they put a roster out that tells you what kind of duty you will have the next day. The roster isn't official until Guard Mount because if someone gets sick, you might have to take over his or her assignment if it has a higher priority than yours. If you are assigned to work the gate, then your duties include waving vehicles on through the gate if they have decals on their vehicles, giving people directions if they are new to the base, and just acting as ambassadors for the Air Force.

The Air Force is changing the job duties. The emphasis will be more on air base security and not so much on law enforcement. But it is still a good starting point if you want to get your foot in the door. You get good training!

# CHAPTER four

## JOB OPPORTUNITIES: LOCAL AND STATE

IN THIS chapter, we will begin to explore many of the hundreds of law enforcement jobs that exist at local and state levels. You will find descriptions of the jobs, qualifications, selections processes, and training. You'll also learn about opportunities in the field of corrections. We have also included information on how to find out who is hiring for these positions.

**SO FAR** we have taken an overview of law enforcement work and discussed the requirements of candidates seeking law enforcement positions. Now we will look at many of the hundreds of career opportunities that exist in the field. This chapter will cover opportunities in:

- Municipal and Metropolitan Police Departments
- Sheriff Departments
- State Law Enforcement Agencies
- Campus Police Departments

To give you an idea of the variety of law enforcement positions that exist, consult the partial listing in the box below. We will look closely at the qualifications, job descriptions, and training for many of these jobs and tell you how and where to apply for them. During your job search, you should consult the Internet guide in Appendix A and the list of helpful publications found in Appendix C.

| | | |
|---|---|---|
| Arson Investigator | Document Specialist | Police Surgeon |
| Ballistics Expert | Evidence Technician | Polygraph Operator |
| Booking Officer | FBI Special Agent | Professor |
| Border Patrol Officer | Fingerprint Expert | Psychiatric Advisor |
| Chaplain | Firearms Instructor | Public Safety Director |
| Chief of Police | Forensic Scientist | Radio Communications |
| Communications Officer | Gaming Enforcement Agent | Records Management Director |
| Community Service Officer | Gang Investigator | Security Specialist |
| Conservation Officer | Intelligence Officer | Secret Service Agent |
| Correctional Officer | Investigator | Sheriff |
| Crime Lab Technician | Juvenile Specialist | Street Crimes Specialist |
| Customs Officer | K-9 Handler | S.W.A.T. |
| Deputy | Narcotics Agent | Training Director |
| Deputy Chief | Operations Specialist | Treasury Agent |
| Detective | Patrol Officer | Trooper |
| Detention Officer | Photographer | Undercover Operative |
| Dir. of Scientific Services | Police Attorney | U.S. Marshal |
| Dir. of Training | Police Psychologist | Witness Protection Agent |

## MUNICIPAL AND METROPOLITAN POLICE DEPARTMENTS

The majority of those working in law enforcement are city or county uniform police officers. They number more than 500,000, and hold jobs in over 12,000 agencies across the country. These are the officers that the public knows—we see them directing traffic, writing tickets, and patrolling neighborhoods. What we don't see are the many other duties of these men and women. Police officers investigate crimes, write reports, issue special licenses and permits, and testify in court. While in very large metropolitan agencies there are specialists, most police officers have a wide range of responsibilities, making each day different from the one before.

## Job Opportunities

Smaller municipal police departments range in size from one officer to less than 100. They are headed by a chief of police, who is in charge of the patrol, detective, and communications divisions. In these three divisions work patrol officers, detectives, and dispatchers. Due to the small structure, there are limited opportunities for employment and advancement. However, many of these departments are hiring. Check out the list on page 73 for more information on finding out where the jobs are.

Large metropolitan departments employ anywhere from 100 to thousands of officers. Their structure is similar to that of municipal departments, but because of the number of employees, they can offer specialty positions such as community policing officers, narcotics agents, and computer specialists. The size of these departments, coupled with their locations in large cities with often-higher crime rates, means that they have many more opportunities for employment and advancement.

Whether you take a job with a municipal or metropolitan police department, there is a good chance you will start out in the patrol division. Patrol officers do exactly what their title implies: patrol a designated area, usually by car or on foot, and in some cases by motorcycle, bicycle, or horseback. You may work alone or with a partner, depending on the nature of your assignment and the size of the police force. Typically, you'll work 40-hour weeks on rotating shifts, not including overtime or required court appearances. In some cases, you may be offered the chance to work an extra shift, depending on the needs of the department.

Some of the duties of a patrol officer include:

- traffic control
- crowd control
- response to 911 calls
- fingerprinting
- securing the scene of a crime

- interviewing witnesses, victims, and suspects
- handling domestic disturbances
- making traffic stops
- subduing and arresting suspects

**JUST THE FACTS**

Baseball is the only sport in which moonlighting policemen are on the payrolls. These officers are paid as part-time employees of Major League Baseball to help with security.

## Qualifications

Although requirements for becoming a police officer vary among police departments, typically you must be a U.S. citizen between the ages of 18 and 29 at the time of appointment. Other possible requirements include:

- a valid driver's license and a good driving record
- a high school diploma or GED
- a college degree (or a specified number of college credits)
- residency in the city or county in which you apply
- no felony convictions

Some departments will ask that you have some college credits, and others will want you to have an associate degree or higher. Some will allow a misdemeanor record, according to what crimes were committed, and others will ask for a clean record. Stringent qualifications are necessary because the responsibilities of the job are serious: you will be asked to safeguard the lives and property of citizens, to protect every citizen's constitutional rights, and to enforce the law fairly. Police officers are held to a higher standard.

## Selection Process

Law enforcement agencies across the United States are using tougher standards than they did in the past when hiring new officers. Situations like the

Rodney King case in California and similar cases across the nation have helped create an atmosphere in which the public can be mistrustful of the police. Politics get involved when candidates and public officials try to win votes by promising to change things. Police chiefs and their departments feel the pressure, and they are more concerned than ever about departmental liability and the actions of their officers. The application process is discussed in detail in Chapter 6. Most agencies will ask that you undergo some, if not all, of the following:

- written examination
- physical agility testing
- psychological testing
- polygraph examination
- background investigation
- oral interview sessions

## Training

After you make it through the selection process and you've been offered the job, your next goals are to pass the training program in the academy and make it through the probationary period. If your agency puts you through an academy program, you'll learn all the skills you need to make it as a police officer. If your agency does not have an academy, you may be sponsored by your police department (meaning they pay the bills for your training) and sent to a regional academy. For example, the Plymouth Regional Police Academy in Massachusetts provides training for basic municipal police recruits for municipal police departments in the southeast part of the state, in Cape Cod and in the Islands.

The exact curriculum and number of hours of instruction may vary among different police academies, but they usually address similar subject and skill areas. Your classroom training may start with an overview of the U.S. criminal justice system. This may cover both law enforcement agencies and the courts, and probably includes a look at both the history of policing and modern policing strategies.

You will learn about constitutional law and penal, civil, juvenile, and vehicle/traffic law. You'll also receive instruction on police discretionary powers and the use of physical force. The more personal side of policing—interacting with the public, handling the pressures of the job, and so forth—will be handled under the classroom topics of community relations and public service, police ethics, and stress management.

Skills training is a major portion of a police academy course. You will become adept in the use of firearms and other police weapons and equipment. Physical fitness training will become a priority in your life. It is necessary to be in top physical condition to be able to excel in self-defense, physical restraint, and arrest techniques training.

In recent years, community colleges in many states have started offering police academy training, sometimes called "open enrollment academies." The subjects and training offered in these settings are the same as what you'd find in the departmental police academies, if not better. Students may be required to take college courses in areas such as English composition or basic criminal law as prerequisites to the academy course. The main differences, however, are that you'll be taking on the financial responsibility yourself and that you wont necessarily have a job in law enforcement waiting for you upon graduation. Usually the bill includes registration and administrative fees, plus costs for books, equipment, weapons, uniforms, and other gear. (Costs vary by institution, but plan on a total of roughly $1,400 to $2,500.) What you get in return is certification as a police officer and proof that you've got what it takes to do the job. This is what you will need for those instances when you apply to a department that requires you to be certified before they will hire you. Find out the requirements of the agency you want to work for before you enroll in one of these programs. To find out about open enrollment academies, contact the admissions director of the community college nearest to you or ask your local police department.

Your training is not really considered complete by most departments without OJT (on-the-job-training) by a field training officer. Field training is conducted after you've finished the police academy program, though some academies consider it the final phase of their program. On the whole, departments include the time you spend in field training as part of the probationary employment period for new officers. Its main purpose is to provide practical experience in policing. When you participate in either formal field training programs or supervised on-the-job training, departments have the chance to gauge your technical skills, your knowledge of the law and of the procedures you learned in the classroom, and how you interact with the public. They can see if their time, money, and training have paid off. Field training officers who do not feel comfortable with your knowledge and performance can recommend that the department either retrain you or fire you.

## Finding a Job

To find out about the latest job openings in your community, call your local police department's non-emergency number. They may also advertise in local newspapers and on websites such as www.lawenforcementjobs.com and www.policeemployment.com. The largest municipal and metropolitan agencies have the most job opportunities. Below is a list these agencies, beginning with the largest, with contact information. Numbers of full-time sworn personnel were taken from U.S. Department of Justice figures for 1997.

**NEW YORK CITY POLICE DEPT.**

1 Police Plaza, 14th floor
New York, NY 10038
(212) 374-5410
www.ci.nyc.ny.us/html/nypd/home.html
Full-time sworn personnel (OFC): 38,328

**CHICAGO POLICE DEPT.**

1121 S. State Street
Cook County
Chicago, IL 60605
(312) 747-5501
www.ci.chi.il.us/CommunityPolicing
OFC: 13,271

**LOS ANGELES POLICE DEPT.**

150 N. Los Angeles Street
LA County
Los Angeles, CA 90012
(213) 485-3202
www.lapdonline.org/index.htm
OFC: 9,423

**PHILADELPHIA POLICE DEPT.**

8th and Race Street, Franklin Square
Philadelphia County
Philadelphia, PA 19106
(215) 686-3280
www.phila.gov/departments/police
OFC: 6,782

**HOUSTON POLICE DEPT.**
1200 Travis 16th floor
Harris County
Houston, TX 77002
(713) 308-1600
www.ci.houston.tx.us/department/police
OFC: 5,355

**DETROIT POLICE DEPT.**
1300 Beaubien Street
Wayne County
Detroit, MI 48226
(313) 596-1800
www.ci.detroit.mi.us/police
OFC: 4,070

**WASHINGTON, DC, POLICE DEPT.**
300 Indiana Avenue NW, Room 5080
District of Columbia
Washington, DC 20001
www.mpdc.org/English/Recruiting/PoliceOfficer/htm
OFC: 3,618

**BALTIMORE POLICE DEPT.**
601 E. Fayette Street
Baltimore, MD 21202
(410) 396-2020
www.ci.baltimore.md.us/government/police/police1.htm
OFC: 3,082

**NASSAU COUNTY POLICE DEPT.**
1490 Franklin Avenue
Mineola, NY 11501
(516) 573-7100
www.co.nassau/ny.us/police
OFC: 2,935

**MIAMI-DADE COUNTY POLICE DEPT.**
9105 NW 25th Street
Miami, FL 33172
(305) 471-2100
www.mdpd.metro-dade.com
OFC: 2,920

**DALLAS POLICE DEPT.**
2014 Main Street, Room 506
Dallas County
Dallas, TX 75201
www.ci.dallas.tx.us/dpd
OFC: 2,817

**SUFFOLK COUNTY POLICE DEPT.**
100 Center Drive
Riverhead, NY 11901
(631) 852-2200
www.bern.nais.com/clients/scpd/scpdshp.shtml
OFC: 2,711

**PHOENIX POLICE DEPT.**
620 W. Washington Place
Maricopa County
Phoenix, AZ 85003
(602) 262-6151
www.ci.phoenix.az.us/POLICE/policidx/html
OFC: 2,428

**BOSTON POLICE DEPT.**
1 Schroeder Plaza
Suffolk County
Boston, MA 02120
(617) 343-4200
www.ci.boston.ma.us/police/
OFC: 2,190

**MILWAUKEE POLICE DEPT.**
749 W. State Street
Milwaukee County
Milwaukee, WI 53201
(414) 935-7302
www.milw-police.org/
OFC: 2,151

**SAN FRANCISCO POLICE DEPT.**
850 Bryant Street, Suite 525
San Francisco County
San Francisco, CA 94103
(415) 553-1551
www.ci.sf.ca.us/police/
OFC: 2,006

**SAN DIEGO POLICE DEPT.**
1401 Broadway
San Diego County
San Diego, CA 92101
www.san-diego.ca.us/police/career/index/shtml
OFC: 1,964

**SAN ANTONIO POLICE DEPT.**
214 W. Nueva Street
Bexnar County
San Antonio, TX 78207
(210) 207-7484
www.ci.sat.tx.us/sapd
OFC: 1,867

**CLEVELAND POLICE DEPT.**
1300 Ontario Street
Cuyahoga County
Cleveland, OH 44113
(216) 623-5005
www.clevelandpd.net
OFC: 1,798

**COLUMBUS POLICE DEPT.**
120 Marconi Boulevard
Franklin County
Columbus, OH 43215
(614) 645-4600
www.megavision.net/police/
OFC: 1,726

**LAS VEGAS METROPOLITAN POLICE DEPT.**
400 E. Stewart Avenue
Clark County
Las Vegas, NV 89010
(702) 795-3111
www.lvmp.com
OFC: 1,709

**ISLAND OF OAHU POLICE DEPT.**
801 S. Beretania Street
Honolulu County
Honolulu, HI 96813
(808) 529-3161
www.honolulupd.org
OFC: 1,691

**ATLANTA POLICE DEPT.**
675 Ponce De Leon Avenue
Fulton County
Atlanta, GA 30308
(404) 817-6900
www.atlantapd.org
OFC: 1,612

**BALTIMORE COUNTY POLICE DEPT.**
401 Dosley
Towson, MD 21204
(410) 887-3151
www.co.ba.md.us/bacoweb/services/police/html/police.htm
OFC: 1,608

**ST. LOUIS POLICE DEPT.**
1200 Clark Avenue
St. Louis County
St. Louis, MO 63103
(314) 444-5624
www.co.st-louis.mo.us/police
OFC: 1,600

## SHERIFF DEPARTMENTS

These departments are very similar to municipal police departments, but they have jurisdiction over counties rather than towns or cities. There are more than 3,000 sheriff departments in the United States (compared to more than 13,000 police departments). They share many responsibilities with police officers, such as crime investigation and various types of patrol. In addition, the sheriff department is involved with prison and court operations.

### Job Opportunities

The law enforcement officers hired by the sheriff's office are called deputy sheriffs. The position of deputy is often an "at will" position, meaning that deputies serve at the will of the sheriff. The sheriff, on the other hand, is usually an elected official and serves at the will of the voter.

After being hired as a deputy sheriff, you will be assigned to patrol rural areas or places that aren't served by a local police department. Like police officers, your duties will include patrolling an assigned area in a marked patrol car, and investigating suspicious or criminal activity. You will have all the necessary powers of arrest, search, and seizure. Your main responsibility is the protection of people and property. Some of your more specific job duties will include:

- crowd control
- writing citations for traffic violations on county roads
- emergency first-aid for accident victims or victims of violent crime
- crime scene duties
- fingerprinting
- evidence procurement
- crime scene security
- witness, victim, and suspect interviews
- surveillance work
- undercover work
- service with SWAT units or other specialized details

Deputy sheriffs usually work 40-hour weeks on rotating shifts, and put in extra hours from time to time. Serving extra duty and testifying in court may be necessary at times. Whether you patrol alone or with a partner will depend on the size and needs of your department.

The sheriff's department is responsible for operating, maintaining, and staffing correctional facilities for the county. They also provide security for courthouses and courtrooms. Consequently, you could also:

- serve subpoenas, summonses, warrants and other court orders
- conduct evictions
- escort prisoners to and from correction facilities
- extradite fugitives from other jurisdictions

## Qualifications

Counties have different criteria for hiring deputy sheriffs. In most places, you must be between 21 and 29 years of age, be a U.S. citizen, and have a valid driver's license. You will also need a high school diploma or a General Equivalency Degree (GED). The growing trend, like that for police officers, is for departments to require at least some college credits, if not a degree.

## Selection Process

Sheriff's departments have different selection processes. Some employers will ask that you pass a written exam, while others will only want to see the results of your background investigation and/or personal interview before they hire you. Larger departments will usually require that you go through a more stringent process involving some, if not all, of the following:

- written exams
- physical agility tests
- psychological testing
- physical agility exams
- polygraph testing
- background investigations
- oral interview boards

## Training

The type and amount of training you receive varies from county to county, depending on the size the department and its budget. Smaller departments may opt for on-the-job training under close supervision by a superior officer, while larger departments may have formal training procedures lasting anywhere from six weeks to six months, followed by supervised on-the-job training. All deputy sheriffs are required to meet minimum training standards set forth by each state.

## Finding a Job

To find out about local job openings, call your county employment office. You can also read about departments across the country if you log onto the National Sheriffs Association website, www.sheriffs.org.

You can also check out the fastest growing sheriff's departments in the county for job opportunities. They are listed below, with contact information.

**LOS ANGELES COUNTY, CA**

Los Angeles County Sheriff's Dept.
4700 Ramona Boulevard
Monterey Park, CA 91754
(323) 526-5541
www.la-sheriff.org
Full-time sworn personnel (OFC): 8,014

**COOK COUNTY, IL**

Cook County Sheriff's Office
118 North Clark, Room 1079
Chicago, IL 60602
www.cookcountysheriff.org
(800) 458-1002
OFC: 5,309

**SAN DIEGO COUNTY, CA**

San Diego Sheriff's Office
9621 Ridgehaven Court, P.O. Box 429000
San Diego, CA 92142-9000
(858) 974-2222
www.co.san-diego.ca.us/cnty/cntydepts/safety/sheriff
OFC: 1,700

**PALM BEACH COUNTY, FL**

Palm Beach Sheriff's Office
3228 Gun Club Road
West Palm Beach, FL 33406
(561) 688-3000
www.pbso.org
OFC: 1,620

**RIVERSIDE COUNTY, CA**

Riverside Sheriff's Dept.
7477 Mission Boulevard
Riverside, CA 92509
(888) 564-6773
www.co.riverside.ca.us/sheriff
OFC: 1,357

**BEXAR COUNTY, TX**

Bexar County Sheriff's Dept.
200 N. Comal
San Antonio, TX 78207
(210) 270-6010
www.co.bexar.tx.us/sheriff
OFC: 1,169

### SACRAMENTO COUNTY, CA

Sacramento County Sheriff's Dept.
1000 River Walk Way
Carmichael, CA 95608
(916) 875-0085
www.sacsheriff.com
OFC: 1,155

### SAN BERNARDINO COUNTY, CA

San Bernardino Sheriff's Dept.
655 East Third Street
San Bernadino, CA 92415
(909) 387-0658
www.co.san-bernardino.ca.us/sheriff
OFC: 1,149

### BROWARD COUNTY, FL

Broward Sheriff's Office
2601 West Broward Boulevard
Ft. Lauderdale, FL 33312
(954) 831-8900
www.sheriff.org
OFC: 1,029

### NASSAU COUNTY, NY

Nassau County Police Dept.
1655 Dutch Broadway
Elmont, NY 11003
(516) 573-6500
www.geocities.com/CapitolHill/Lobby/9063
OFC: 1,004

### ORANGE COUNTY, FL

Orange County Sheriff's Office, Human Resources Dept.
2450 W. 33rd Street
Orlando, FL 32839
(407) 836-4070
www.magicnet.net/ocso
OFC: 980

### HILLSBOROUGH COUNTY, FL

Hillsborough County Sheriff's Office
P.O. Box 3371
Tampa, FL 33601
(813) 247-8000
www.hcso.tampa.fl.us
OFC: 937

### ORLEANS PARISH, LA

Orleans Parish Criminal Sheriff's Office
2614 Tulane Avenue
New Orleans, LA 70119
(504) 827-6777
www.opcso.org
OFC: 800

### WAYNE COUNTY, MI

Wayne County Sheriff and Airport Police Local 502
20926 Schoolcraft
Detroit, MI 48223
(313) 534-2307
www.local502.com
OFC: 800

**SUFFOLK COUNTY, NY**

Suffolk County Sheriff's Dept.
100 Center Drive
Riverhead, NY 11901
www.co.suffolk.ny.us/sheriff
(631) 852-2200
OFC: 764

**HAMILTON COUNTY, OH**

Hamilton County Sheriff's Office
Justice Center
1000 Sycamore Street
Cincinnati, OH 45202-1340
(513) 946-6400
www.hcso.org
OFC: 764

**VENTURA COUNTY, CA**

Ventura County Sheriff's Dept.
800 S. Victoria Avenue
Ventura, CA 93009
(805) 654-2311
www.vcsd.org
OFC: 706

**PINELLAS COUNTY, FL**

Office of the Sheriff, Personnel Dept.
10750 Ulmerton Road
Largo, FL 33778
(727) 582-6208
www.co.pinellas.fl.us/sheriff/pcso.htm
OFC: 698

**E. BATON ROUGE PARISH, LA**

East Baton Rouge Sheriff's Office
P.O. Box 3277
Baton Rouge, LA 70821
(225) 389-5000
www.ebrso.org
OFC: 625

## STATE POLICE

Every state has its own system of law enforcement, headed by the attorney general, and broken down into three main areas: the state police, corrections and parole, and conservation and wildlife. The majority of job openings at the state level occur in the police and corrections division, which we will explore below.

Although his or her main responsibility is to ensure public safety on the state's roadways, a highway patrol officer's job also involves many of the same duties as that of a deputy or municipal police officer. They patrol their assigned areas, enforce traffic laws, deal with accidents and other emergencies, and provide safety programs for the public. In communities and counties that do not have a local police force or a large sheriff's department, state troopers are the primary law enforcement agents, investigating crimes such as burglary or assault.

### Job Opportunities

Depending on the state you are in, state troopers go by different names: state trooper, highway patrol officer, state police officer, or state traffic officer. Some specific duties of a state trooper are:

- observing and reporting public safety hazards, such as unsafe driving conditions or roadway obstacles
- investigating conditions and causes of accidents
- appearing in court as witnesses in traffic and criminal cases
- writing reports
- assisting law enforcement officers from other jurisdictions
- conducting driver exams
- monitoring violations of commercial vehicle weight laws
- arresting persons who are driving while intoxicated
- executing search and/or arrest warrants
- enforcing drug laws

### Qualifications

Requirements for this position vary among the states, but usually you must be a U.S. citizen between 21 and 29 years of age at the time of appointment and a resident of the state in which you are applying. Other requirements include:

- a valid driver's license and a good driving record
- a high school diploma or GED
- at least 60 college hours (may be required or merely preferred)
- no felony convictions

### Selection Process

Again, the selection process will vary. At the least, you should expect:

- written testing
- physical agility testing
- psychological testing
- polygraph examination
- drug screening
- background investigation
- medical examination

### Training

Every state that has a state police agency (all but Hawaii) has its own academy. Expect training similar to that given to municipal police officers.

### Finding a Job

State police traditionally request that you contact the troop or district office nearest to your hometown for recruiting information. Consult your phone book for the numbers in your community. You can also check the list of 10 of the fastest growing state departments below. On the Internet, you may find job openings listed on sites such as www.tap.net/~hyslo/poljobs.

**CALIFORNIA HIGHWAY PATROL**
2555 First Avenue
Sacramento, CA 95818
(916) 657-7261

**CONNECTICUT STATE POLICE**
1111 Country Club Road
Middletown, CT 06457
(860) 685-8230

**ILLINOIS STATE HIGHWAY POLICE**
201 East Adams
Springfield, IL 62701
(217) 782-6637

**KENTUCKY STATE POLICE**
Department of Public Safety
919 Versailles Road
Frankfort, KY 40601

**NEW JERSEY STATE POLICE**
P.O. Box 7068, River Road
West Trenton, NJ 08628
(609) 882-2000

**NEW YORK STATE POLICE**
Campus, Public Security Building 22
Albany, NY 12226
(518) 457-2180

**OHIO STATE HIGHWAY PATROL**
660 East Main Street
Columbus, OH 43205
(614) 752-2792

**PENNSYLVANIA STATE POLICE**
1800 Elmerton Avenue
Harrisburg, PA 17110
(717) 787-6941

**TEXAS STATE POLICE**
Department of Public Safety
5805 North Lamar Boulevard
Austin, TX 78752
(512) 465-2000

**WASHINGTON STATE PATROL**
Headquarters Administration Building
Olympia, WA 98504
(360) 753-6540

## CORRECTIONS OFFICER

Corrections is a fast growing job market that is very closely related to the law enforcement field. The reason for this growth in jobs is that law enforcement is putting more criminals in jail. Since 1980, there has been a 40% increase in the prison population, which has in turn led to the building of more jails, prisons, and detention centers. And all of these facilities need corrections officers to operate them.

### Job Opportunities

A corrections officer's primary duty is to guard and supervise prisoners confined to penal institutions. This role doesn't change from facility to facility, but specific duties will, depending on the size and type of institution employing the officer. As with the municipal police, smaller departments are staffed by officers who perform a wide range of duties, while larger ones have officers who specialize in a particular area. In either setting, the corrections officer is charged with maintaining order, enforcing the rules of the institution, ensuring the safety of inmates and fellow officers, and preventing escape.

Unarmed corrections officers are responsible for the direct supervision of inmates. You may be locked in a cellblock alone, or with another officer, to watch 50 to 100 inmates. Here, excellent communication skills work to your advantage. You will routinely search inmates and cells for weapons, drugs, or other illegal items. You will supervise inmates while they work, exercise, eat, and bathe. You will constantly make sure doors, locks, and windows have not been tampered with, and that all are functioning properly. And you will be on alert for any signs of tension or disruptive conduct among inmates that could lead to fighting or riots.

The disciplinary role of a corrections officer is a crucial element of the job. You can't show favoritism in your dealings with inmates and must be prepared to use the appropriate level of force to protect the inmates under your supervision. That may include anything from the use of your voice to hand-to-hand defensive tactics to the use of weapons.

Corrections officers usually work eight-hour shifts, five days a week, with rotating days off. Since security is a 24-hour occupation, be prepared to work late-night hours, weekends, and holidays until you achieve seniority. There are usually overtime hours as well.

**IN THE NEWS**

Kentucky recently passed a law that allows the state's 85 jails to charge inmates up to $50 per day for room and board. The law only applies to prisoners with sentences of one year or less, and it is intended to serve as a deterrent. The chief of the Kentucky Jailers' Association, who lobbied for the new law, says, "Crime doesn't pay . . . [but] maybe criminals should."

## Qualifications

Most institutions ask that you be:

- a minimum of 18 to 21 years old
- a citizen of the United States
- a high school graduate, or the equivalent
- in good health
- a licensed driver

As with other law enforcement departments, the trend in corrections is toward hiring applicants with college educations, especially those who've studied psychology, criminal justice, police science, criminology, or similar subjects. A stable work history is also a plus.

### Selection Process

The selection process may vary considerably among agencies, depending on whether you apply to the county, state, or federal system. Federal requirements are generally the most stringent. (For more information about the federal selection process, see Chapter 5.) At the least, be prepared to pass the following:

- drug screening
- written or oral examinations
- background checks
- psychological examination

### Training

When you are first hired as a corrections officer, you will be considered a probationary employee as you begin training. Federal, state, and local corrections departments use training guidelines set by certain professional organizations, including the American Correctional Association and the American Jail Association. What varies from institution to institution is whether you will first receive on-the-job training or go through a formal training program, such as an academy.

Corrections officers in federal prisons get their training through the Federal Bureau of Prisons at Glynco, Georgia. Within 60 days of being hired, you will be required to complete 120 hours of specialized correctional instruction at Glynco. You need to have 200 hours of formal training within the first year of employment. Once you leave Glynco and are on the job, you will be supervised by more experienced officers in an on-the-job training environment.

Corrections officers hired at the state and local level rely heavily on on-the-job training, though they are required to go through formal training courses mandated by the state. Many state facilities are in the process of developing formal training programs similar to the Federal Bureau of Prisons, and already have special training academies.

Training usually includes instruction on institution rules, regulations, and operations. Other topics to be covered are:

- constitutional law
- custody and security procedures
- fire and safety
- CPR training
- crisis intervention
- inmate behavior
- contraband control
- report writing
- firearms and hand-to-hand self-defense instruction
- physical fitness training

At all institutions—federal, state, and local—it is common for corrections officers to participate in formal training courses after being employed for a period of time. Generally, this in-service continuing education is designed to teach officers new ideas and techniques or certain specialized skills, often for job advancement.

### Finding a Job

Start by consulting the list on the following pages of contact information for every state corrections department. Often, job listings are included on their websites. Also on the web, look up www.corrections.com. From this site, you'll find links to other corrections-related sites such as those maintained by the American Correctional Association and the American Jail Association. You can purchase an exhaustive list of facilities entitled *Directory of Juvenile and Adult Correctional Departments*, published by the American Correctional Association (4380 Forbes Boulevard, Lanham, Maryland 20706-4322; 1-800-222-5646). Also worth contacting is the American Jail Association, 2053 Day Road, Suite 100, Hagerstown, Maryland 21740; (301) 790-3930.

**ALABAMA DEPT. OF CORRECTIONS AND HUMAN SERVICES**
101 South Union Street
Montgomery, AL
(334) 353-3870
www.agencies.state.al.us/doc

**ALASKA DEPT. OF CORRECTIONS**
4500 Diplomacy Drive, Room 207
Anchorage, AK 99508
(907) 269-7450
www.correct.state.ak.us

**ARIZONA DEPT. OF CORRECTIONS**
1601 W. Jefferson
Phoenix, AZ 85007
(602) 542-5497
www.adc.state.az.us:81

**ARKANSAS DEPT. OF CORRECTIONS**
P.O. Box 8707
Pine Bluff, AR 71611
(870) 247-6200
www.state.ar.us/doc

**CALIFORNIA YOUTH AND ADULT CORRECTIONAL AGENCY**
1100 11th Street, Suite 400
Sacramento, CA 95814
(916) 323-6001
www.bdcorr.ca.gov

**COLORADO DEPT. OF CORRECTIONS**
2862 South Circle Drive, Suite 400
Colorado Springs, CO 80906
(719) 579-9580
www.doc.state.co.us/index.html

**CONNECTICUT DEPT. OF CORRECTIONS**
24 Wolcott Hill Road
Wethersfield, CT 06109
(860) 692-7481
www.state.st.us/doc

**DELAWARE DEPT. OF CORRECTIONS**
245 Nckee Road
Smyrna, DE 19904
(302) 739-5601
www.state.de.us/correct/ddoc/default.htm

**FLORIDA DEPT. OF CORRECTIONS**
2601 Blair Stone Road
Tallahassee, FL 32399
(850) 488-7480
www.foc.state.fl.us

**GEORGIA DEPT. OF CORRECTIONS**
2 Martin Luther King Drive, SE Floyd Bldg.
Atlanta, GA 30334
(404) 656-6002
www.dcor.state.ga.us

**HAWAII DEPT. OF PUBLIC SAFETY**
919 Ala Moana Boulevard
Honolulu, HI 96814
(808) 587-1350
www.state.hi.us/icsd/psd.html

**IDAHO DEPT. OF CORRECTIONS**
500 South 10th Street
Boise, ID 83709
(208) 658-2000
www.corr.state.id.us

**ILLINOIS DEPT. OF CORRECTIONS**
1301 Concordia Court
Springfield, IL 62794
(217) 522-2666
www.idoc.state.il.us

**INDIANA DEPT. OF CORRECTIONS**
302 W. Washington Street, Room E334
IGCS
Indianapolis, IN 46204
(317) 232-5711
www.state.in.us/indcorrection

**IOWA DEPT. OF CORRECTIONS**
420 Kes Way
Des Moines, IA 50309
(515) 242-5703
www.state.ia.us/government/doc/index.html

**KANSAS DEPT. OF CORRECTIONS**
900 SW Jackson, 4th floor
Topeka, KS 66612
(785) 296-3317
www.ink.org/public/kdoc

**KENTUCKY DEPT. OF CORRECTIONS**
State Office Building
Frankfort, KY 40601
(502) 564-4726
www.cor.state.ky.us/factsnfigures/ADP.htm

**LOUISIANA DEPT. OF PUBLIC SAFETY AND CORRECTIONS**
504 Mayflower Street, Bldg. 1
Baton Rouge, LA 70802
(504) 342-6741
www.state.la.us

**MAINE DEPT. OF CORRECTIONS**
State House Stattion #111
Augusta, ME 04333
(207) 287-4360
www.janus.state.me.us/corrections

**MARYLAND DEPT. OF PUBLIC SAFETY AND CORRECTIONAL SERVICES**
300 E. Joppa Road, Suite 1000
Towson, MD 21286
(410) 339-5000
www.dpscs.state.md.us

**MASSACHUSETTS EXECUTIVE OFFICE OF PUBLIC SAFETY**
1 Ashburton Place, Room 2133
Boston, MA 02108
(617) 727-7775
www.magnet.state.ma.us/doc

**MICHIGAN DEPT. OF CORRECTIONS**
206 E. Michigan Avenue
Lansing, MI 48909
(517) 373-0720
www.state.mi.us/mdoc/IE1.html

**MINNESOTA DEPT. OF CORRECTIONS**
1450 Energy Park Drive, Suite 200
St. Paul, MN 55108
(651) 642-0282
www.corr.state.mn.us

**MISSISSIPPI DEPT. OF CORRECTIONS**
723 N. President Street
Jackson, MS 39202
(662) 359-5600
www.mdoc.state.ms.us

**MISSOURI DEPT. OF CORRECTIONS**
2729 Plaza Drive
Jefferson City, MO 65102
(573) 751-2389
www.corrections.state.mo.us

**MONTANA DEPT. OF CORRECTIONS**
1539 11th Avenue
Helena, MT 59620
(406) 444-3930
www.state.mt.us/cor/index.htm

**NEBRASKA DEPT. OF CORRECTIONAL SERVICES**
Folsom and West Prospector Place, Building 15
Lincoln, NE 68509
(402) 471-2654
www.corrections.state.ne.us

**NEVADA DEPT. OF PRISONS**
5500 Snyder Avenue
Carson City, NV 89702
(775) 887-3216
www.state.nv.us/prisons

**NEW HAMPSHIRE DEPT. OF CORRECTIONS**
P.O. Box 1806
Concord, NH 03302
(603) 271-5606
www.state.nh.us/doc/

**NEW JERSEY DEPT. OF CORRECTIONS**
P.O. Box 863
Trenton, NJ 08625
(609) 292-4036
www.state.nj.us/corrections

### NEW MEXICO DEPT. OF CORRECTIONS

Highway 14
Santa Fe, NM 87502
(505) 827-8709
www.state.nm.us/corrections

### NEW YORK DEPT. OF CORRECTIONAL SERVICES

1220 Washington Avenue, Building 2
Albany, NY 12226
(518) 457-8126
www.dpca.state.ny.us

### NORTH CAROLINA DEPT. OF CORRECTIONS

214 W. Jones Street
Raleigh, NC 27603
(919) 733-4926
www.doc.state.nc.us

### NORTH DAKOTA DEPT. OF CORRECTIONS AND REHABILITATION

P.O. Box 1898
Bismark, ND 58502
www.state.nd.us/docr

### OHIO DEPT. OF REHABILITATION AND CORRECTIONS

1050 Freeway Drive N.
Columbus, OH 43229
(614) 752-1164
www.ocjs.state.oh.us

### OKLAHOMA DEPT. OF CORRECTIONS

3400 Martin Luther King Jr. Avenue
Oklahoma City, OK 73136
(405) 425-2500
www.doc.state.ok.us

### OREGON DEPT. OF CORRECTIONS

2575 Center Street NE
Salem, OR 97310
(503) 945-0920
www.doc.state.or.us

### PENNSYLVANIA DEPT. OF CORRECTIONS

P.O. Box 598
Camp Hill, PA 17001
(717) 975-4860
www.cor.state.pa.us

### RHODE ISLAND DEPT. OF CORRECTIONS

40 Howard Avenue
Cranston, RI 02920
(401) 462-2611
www.doc.state.ri.us

### SOUTH CAROLINA DEPT. OF CORRECTIONS

4444 Broad River Road
P.O. Box 21787
Columbia, SC 29221
(803) 896-8555
www.state.sc.us/scdc

**SOUTH DAKOTA DEPT. OF CORRECTIONS**
c/o 500 E. Capital Avenue
3200 E. Highway 34
Pierre, SD 57501
(605) 773-3478
www.state.sd.us/corrections.html

**TENNESSEE DEPT. OF CORRECTIONS**
320 Sixth Avenue N, 4th floor
Nashville, TN 37243
(615) 741-2071
www.state.tn.us/corrections

**TEXAS DEPT. OF CRIMINAL JUSTICE**
Spur 59 off Highway 75N
Huntsville, TX 77340
(409) 294-2101
www.tdcj.state.tx.us

**UTAH DEPT. OF CORRECTIONS**
6100 S. Fashion Boulevard
Murray, UT 84107
(801) 265-5500
www.cr.ex.state.ut.us

**VERMONT DEPT. OF CORRECTIONS**
103 S. Main Street
Waterbury, VT 05671
(802) 241-2442
www.public.doc.state.vt.us

**VIRGINIA DEPT. OF CORRECTIONS**
6900 Atmore Drive
Richmond, VA 23225
(804) 674-3119
www.cns.state.va.us/doc

**WASHINGTON DEPT. OF CORRECTIONS**
P.O. Box 41102
Olympia, WA 98504
(360) 753-0388
www.wa.gov/doc

**WEST VIRGINIA DIVISION OF CORRECTIONS**
112 California Avenue, Building 4, Room 300
Charleston, WV 25305
(304) 558-2037
www.state.wv.us/wvdoc/default.htm

**WISCONSIN DEPT. OF CORRECTIONS**
149 E. Wilson Street
Madison, WI 53707
(608) 266-4548
www.wi-doc.com

**WYOMING DEPT. OF CORRECTIONS**
700 W. 21st Street
Cheyenne, WY 82002
(307) 777-7405
www.doc.state.wy.us/corrections.html

## Online Corrections Connections

- Correctional Education Association—information for those interested in the field and for those already working in corrections. Provides links to other sites of interest. [www.sunsite.unc.edu/icea]
- Corrections—a comprehensive website that serves as a home page for many other associations, such as the American Correctional Association and the American Jail Association. Many State Corrections Departments are also linked, and they provide job listings. [www.corrections.com]
- Federal Bureau of Prisons—facts and research related to the federal prison system, including an overview of the organization and its regional offices and facilities. [www.bop.gov]
- International Association of Correctional Officers (IACO)—non-profit organization that is dedicated to serving the professional advancement of correctional officers; includes information about becoming a member and/or subscribing to IACO publications. [www.acsp.uic.edu/iaco/about.htm]
- National Institute of Corrections—an agency of the Federal Bureau of Prisons, the NIC website contains information on corrections practice and policy, e-mail discussions on a variety of corrections-related subjects, downloadable publications, and links to other websites. [www.nicic.org/inst]
- Prisons—a comprehensive website which includes employment opportunities, news relating to corrections issues, a bookstore, and newsgroup postings for participating in discussions on various corrections-related topics. [www.prisons.com]

## CAMPUS POLICE DEPARTMENTS

If you read any of the college guides suggested in Chapter 2, you may have noticed that colleges and universities are rated against each other in a number of ways. As colleges compete for students (and their money), they are more aware than ever of the need to provide a campus that is not only a great learning environment, but is also safe and relatively crime-free. The campus police department is charged with the latter as its mission.

## Job Opportunities

Although campus police departments are small, there are hundreds of them throughout the United States. They are headed by a chief of police, and staffed by police or public safety officers. Larger departments, such as the one at Cornell University in Ithaca, New York, hire officers who specialize in different areas, such as telecommunications.

## Qualifications

Job qualifications are similar to those for state police officers. Although there is some variation between departments, most campus police applicants must:

- hold an associate's or bachelor's degree
- be 21 years of age
- be a resident of the state in which you are applying
- have at least three years of job experience
- possess a valid driver's license

## Selection Process

This process is also similar to that of state police departments. Applicants must first submit a cover letter and resume to the department. Some larger universities also have applications that are required of applicants for any type of campus employment. Then, written exams (possibly the Civil Service exam), physical agility tests, oral interviews, background investigations, and medical and psychological tests are given.

### JUST THE FACTS

The Campus Security Act, also referred to as the Cleary Act, was signed into law in 1990. Named for a Lehigh University student who was murdered in her dorm room, the Cleary Act requires schools to publicly disclose three years of campus security statistics and basic security policies.

## Training

Basic training usually takes place at a state police academy. Once this is complete, there is a probationary period during which officers receive on-the-job training.

## Finding a Job

Many of the Web sites listed in Appendix A list job opportunities on college and university campuses. For instance, www.lawenforcementjob.com has listings of jobs by state. You can read job descriptions, qualifications and testing requirements, and application procedures, and also get contact information.

### Other Good Sources of Employment Information

| Web site | Maintained by |
| --- | --- |
| www.campuspolice.com | University and College Police Association |
| www.iaclea.org | International Association of Campus Law Enforcement |
| www.campussafety.org | Security on Campus, Inc. |

### THE INSIDE TRACK

**Who:** Gary Margolis

**What:** Chief of Police

**Where:** University of Vermont; former Training Coordinator at the Vermont Police Academy

**How Long:** Over two years

**Degree:** Bachelor of Science (Biochemistry), University of Vermont; Masters in Education, University of Vermont; Ed.D. (Doctor of Education) candidate

When I was in college, I got a degree in biochemistry because that was what interested me at the time. During school, I worked for student security, which piqued my interest in a career in law enforcement. My degree taught me to think analytically, and those skills are useful for crime investigation, which can get technical. If I had taken a job in that field, I would have missed the human relations and public service aspects of what I do now, which are the most important.

Now, when I interview job applicants, I look for people with good interpersonal skills, and who believe in public service. People who don't have these skills can get themselves into trouble and give the police a bad name. The most complaints we get concerning our officers have to do with not being aware of people's emotions. When we deal with the public, it is often with someone in some sort of crisis. I need officers who have some life experience and maturity so they can relate well to these people.

Many people want to get into policing without being aware of how people-oriented the job is. Your success as an officer is based on how well you get along with others, so I am looking for this quality from those I interview. I can always teach someone how to fill out a police report; what I can't teach is the human relations side of the work.

I also need officers who are as interested in education as they are in enforcement. It is our duty to be dedicated to crime prevention, which is educational by nature. The police are often called upon to answer questions about home and personal security. We even instruct the public on how to be sure children's car seats are installed properly.

# CHAPTER five

## FEDERAL LAW ENFORCEMENT AGENCIES

IN THIS chapter, we will explore law enforcement positions at the federal level. As with jobs at the municipal and state levels, you will read descriptions of the most popular federal jobs and the responsibilities of these positions. Details about the hiring process, minimum requirements, and testing procedures for all of these positions are also included.

**ACCORDING TO** the U.S. Department of Justice, there were 83,143 full-time law enforcement officers working for the federal government in 1998, up over 11% from 1996. This growth rate looks as if it will continue. While there are seven departments of the federal government who hire law enforcement personnel, the majority of the jobs available are in the Department of Justice and the Treasury Department. This chapter will focus primarily on those jobs, but will also give you information about positions such as those in the Forest Service (through the Department of Agriculture) and the National Park Service (through the Department of Interior).

Once you are hired by a federal agency, you will receive general law enforcement training, most likely through the Federal Law Enforcement

Training Center in Glynco, Georgia, as well as specialized training specifically geared for your type of work. Whatever their missions or jurisdictions, these agencies frequently help each other out with criminal investigations or special projects, including emergencies.

### Largest Employers of Federal Officers Who Are Authorized to Carry Firearms and Make Arrests

| Agency | Number of Officers |
|---|---|
| Immigration and Naturalization Service | 16,552 |
| Bureau of Prisons | 12,587 |
| FBI | 11,285 |
| U.S. Customs Service | 10,539 |

Source: U.S. Department of Justice Bureau of Justice Statistics—March 2000

## DIFFERENCES IN FEDERAL EMPLOYMENT

While many of the federal law enforcement positions are similar to local and state ones, there are a few major differences to consider when applying to the federal government. These include working through the Office of Personnel Management (OPM), and the possibility of relocation once you have secured a position. Both topics are detailed below.

## OFFICE OF PERSONNEL MANAGEMENT

Many job searches at the federal level begin with the Office of Personnel Management (OPM). While some federal agencies have the authority to test and hire applicants directly, most work through the OPM, which accepts applications, administers the appropriate written tests, and then submits an eligibility list of qualified candidates to the agency for consideration. For example, if you want a job with the Bureau of Alcohol, Tobacco, and

Firearms (ATF), you'll have to wait until you see a specific vacancy announcement posted through the OPM, then go through the office to start the application process. (If you already work for a federal agency, you may be able to apply directly to another agency rather than go through the OPM.)

The OPM operates Federal Job Information/Testing Centers in major metropolitan areas across the country. When written tests are required by an agency that works through the OPM, these tests generally will be given at these centers.

You can find out about current job openings and request the application forms you'll need when you contact the OPM. Not only will they provide access to federal, state, and local government job listings, but they also have private sector listings. This is where you'll find the most current information, because it is updated daily and is available every day, 24 hours a day.

There are several ways to get information from OPM, the easiest being through their website at www.opm.gov. At this site, you can read answers to frequently asked questions, read about changes that are affecting government employees, read and download or print some of the forms you may need, and get some background information about the OPM. You can also contact them at (912) 757-3000, TDD (912) 744-2299, or by modem at (912) 757-3100. If you can access sites through the Telnet program, you may reach the OPM at FJOB.MAIL.OPM.GOV.

The OPM also operates two other sites, which are most important for job hunters: www.usacareers.opm.gov and www.usajobs.opm.gov. They are both linked to the main site, so you can access them with one click from www.opm.gov. The first site is for career planning and development. You must subscribe to gain access, but if you want a law enforcement career at the federal level, it is probably worth it. They provide a demo of their services to help you decide. The USACareers site is designed for self-assessment, career planning, and job searching. Through various tests, you can determine your strengths and weaknesses as a job candidate. Then, specific training courses are suggested to improve or eliminate your weaknesses. USACareers also provides a career exploration area that covers many law enforcement positions. Here, you can gain access to "insider" information regarding jobs that may interest you. Finally, there are listings of over 4,000 jobs.

Employment opportunities are also listed—with the full text of the job announcement—at www.usajobs.opm.gov. Once you have read the application process for a specific job, you can access an online application that may be used to create a resume. Once you create it, you can submit it electronically or save it to their system to retrieve and edit for future use. Through this site, and the USACareers site, the OPM has made the process of applying for a federal law enforcement position easier than ever.

Hiring announcements posted for federal job vacancies—by the OPM or directly from a hiring agency—let you know exactly what you'll need to apply. For most federal jobs, you can apply using a resume, a form known as the Optional Application for Federal Employment (available online through the OPM), or some similar kind of written statement.

Federal jobs are classified to indicate the experience, salary level, and other features of the job. These classifications are known as "grades." With your application, you usually need to write in the job title, the announcement number of the job, and the grade(s) assigned to the job. Whatever paperwork you submit must contain all the information that is requested in the job vacancy announcement and on the Optional Application form.

## Relocation

There will be times in your career as a federal law enforcement agent when you may be shuffled from one end of the country to the other, or even overseas, to meet the needs of your department. This is a serious consideration when looking into federal employment. Although most agencies try to accommodate your preferences as to where you want to live, you can and should expect to be asked to move, especially early in your career. As one official with the FBI commented:

> If you originally applied at the San Francisco field office you can bet that won't be where you'll go for your first assignment. We almost never send you back to the field office where you first applied for your first assignment.

Form Approved
OMB No. 3206-0219

# OPTIONAL APPLICATION FOR FEDERAL EMPLOYMENT - OF 612

You may apply for most jobs with a resume, this form, or other written format. If your resume or application does not provide all the information requested on this form and in the job vacancy announcement, you may lose consideration for a job.

| 1 Job title in announcement | | 2 Grade(s) applying for | 3 Announcement number |
|---|---|---|---|
| 4 Last name | First and middle names | | 5 Social Security Number<br>- - |
| 6 Mailing address | | | 7 Phone numbers (include area code)<br>Daytime ( ) |
| City | State | ZIP Code | Evening ( ) |

## WORK EXPERIENCE

8 Describe your paid and nonpaid work experience related to the job for which you are applying. Do **not** attach job descriptions.

1) Job title (if Federal, include series and grade)

| From (MM/YY) | To (MM/YY) | Salary<br>$ | per | Hours per week |
|---|---|---|---|---|
| Employer's name and address | | | | Supervisor's name and phone number<br>( ) |

Describe your duties and accomplishments

2) Job title (if Federal, include series and grade)

| From (MM/YY) | To (MM/YY) | Salary<br>$ | per | Hours per week |
|---|---|---|---|---|
| Employer's name and address | | | | Supervisor's name and phone number<br>( ) |

Describe your duties and accomplishments

9 May we contact your current supervisor?

YES NO Ë If we need to contact your current supervisor before making an offer, we will contact you first.

## EDUCATION

10 Mark highest level completed. **Some HS** **HS/GED** **Associate** **Bachelor** **Master** **Doctoral**

11 Last high school (HS) or GED school. Give the school's name, city, State, ZIP Code (if known), and year diploma or GED received.

12 Colleges and universities attended. Do **not** attach a copy of your transcript unless requested.

| | Name / City, State, ZIP Code | Total Credits Earned: Semester | Total Credits Earned: Quarter | Major(s) | Degree - (if any) | Year Received |
|---|---|---|---|---|---|---|
| 1) | | | | | | |
| 2) | | | | | | |
| 3) | | | | | | |

## OTHER QUALIFICATIONS

13 **Job-related** training courses (give title and year). **Job-related** skills (other languages, computer software/hardware, tools, machinery, typing speed, etc. **Job-related** certificates and licenses (current only). **Job-related** honors, awards, and special accomplishments(publications, memberships in professional/honor societies, leadership activities, public speaking, and performance awards.) Give dates, but do **not** send documents unless requested.

## GENERAL

14 Are you a U.S. citizen? **YES** **NO** Give the country of your citizenship.

15 Do you claim veterans' preference? **NO** **YES** Mark your claim of 5 or 10 points below.

**5 points** Attach your DD 214 or other proof. **10 points** Attach an *Application for 10-Point Veterans' Preference* (SF 15) and proof required.

16 Were you ever a Federal civilian employee?

**NO** **YES** For highest civilian grade give:

| Series | Grade | From (MM/YY) | To (MM/ |
|---|---|---|---|
| | | | |

17 Are you eligible for reinstatement based on career or career-conditional Federal status?

**NO** **YES** If requested, attach SF 50 proof.

## APPLICANT CERTIFICATION

18 **I certify** that, to the best of my knowledge and belief, all of the information on and attached to this application is true, correct, complete and made in good faith. **I understand** that false or fraudulent information on or attached to this application may be grounds for not hiring me or firing me after I begin work, and may b punishable by fine or imprisonment. **I understand** that any information I give may be investigated.

**SIGNATURE** **DATE SIGNED**

While federal employees work in all 50 states and many foreign countries, as of June 1996, about half of all federal officers took assignments in:

- California (11,868)
- Texas (11,059)
- the District of Columbia (7,241)
- New York (6,988)
- Florida (5,343)
- Delaware (93) and New Hampshire (67)

## THE U.S. DEPARTMENT OF JUSTICE

The Department of Justice, under the leadership of the U.S. Attorney General, employs thousands of lawyers, agents, and investigators. The department directs some of the most challenging law enforcement organizations in the federal government, including the INS, FBI, DEA, Bureau of Prisons, and the U.S. Marshals Service.

### U.S. Immigration and Naturalization Service (INS)

The INS is home to the largest force of armed agents, surpassing the Bureau of Prisons and the FBI. From 1996 to 1998, the INS increased its agents 42% from 5,441 to 7,714. National concerns over immigration led to this increase and the hiring is continuing.

The INS enforces and regulates federal laws regarding the immigration and naturalization of non-U.S. citizens. The duties of INS agents include the apprehension and deportation of persons who are trying to enter this country illegally or who have already arrived illegally. They also include criminal investigations, port-of-entry inspection duties, and background investigations on persons applying for U.S. citizenship. Employees of the INS are assigned as border patrol agents, INS special Agents, or INS immigration inspectors.

### Border Patrol Agent

A border patrol agent is one of many uniformed law enforcement officers assigned to guard the borders of the United States—roughly 8,000 miles of land and coastal territory. This agent's chief duty is to detect and prevent the smuggling or entry of illegal aliens into the United States.

Most of a border patrol agent's time is taken up with surveillance and search efforts. Assignments could include combing miles of rough, desolate territory using specially equipped pursuit vehicles: cars, jeeps, helicopters, other aircraft, or patrol boats. To help out, ground points are set up with sensor equipment that sound alarms at stationary duty posts when motion is detected.

Good detective skills are a necessity because agents are expected to detect signs of illegal entry, including footprints, tire tracks, and slashed or broken fences. They also investigate leads, conduct routine inquiries to uncover smuggling operations, and check the citizenship and immigration status of farm and ranch workers. Border patrol agents also set up highway traffic stops and search public transportation sites and vehicles (buses, trucks, trains, airplanes and boats) to find illegal aliens.

Other duties include:

- assisting in the criminal prosecution or deportation of illegal aliens in your custody
- assisting in the criminal prosecution of suspects involved in smuggling illegal aliens
- assisting in court proceedings regarding petitions for citizenship

#### *Qualifications*

Applicants for border patrol agent positions must be U.S. citizens who are at least 21 but under 37 years of age at the time of appointment. You will need to pass a written civil service examination administered by the OPM, a personal interview, a physical exam (including vision and hearing tests), and a background investigation. Work experience is required, either paid or voluntary, although a full four-year course of college undergraduate study may be substituted for work experience.

A key requirement for active border patrol agents is the ability to read and speak Spanish at a good to excellent level. If you have this ability at the time you apply, you will be given additional credit in the hiring process; otherwise, you will have to meet this requirement by the time you complete a one-year probationary period on the job. Border patrol agents are usually assigned first to the southwest states bordering Mexico: California, Arizona, New Mexico, or Texas.

### *Training*

Border patrol trainees participate in an 18-week training program at the Border Patrol Academy located at the Federal Law Enforcement Training Center in Glynco, Georgia. This training covers subject areas such as immigration and naturalization laws, criminal law, tracking methods, pursuit driving, arrest techniques, and firearms.

### *Finding a Job*

You can receive more information from the U.S. Border Patrol office at 425 I Street NW, Washington, DC, 20536. The first step in applying for a job is to take the appropriate civil service examination given by the OPM. To find out when and where the test is administered, contact an OPM office, or the INS directly at www.ins.usdoj.gov, or at their regional offices:

**WESTERN REGION**

Terminal Island
San Pedro, CA 90731

**NORTHERN REGION**

Federal Building
Fort Snelling
Twin Cities, MN 55111

**SOUTHERN REGION**

Skyline Center, Building C
311 North Stemmons Freeway
Dallas, TX 75207

**EASTERN REGION**

Federal Building
Elmwood Avenue
Burlington, VT 05401

## INS Special Agents

Special agents are non-uniformed officers who plan and conduct investigations designed to uncover violations of criminal and statutory laws regulated by the INS. They gather information and evidence by reviewing public and private records and immigration documents, as well as by questioning informants and witnesses and interrogating suspects.

Special agents may get the chance to set up complex surveillance and undercover operations. When their operations are successful, and suspects are caught in the act of a criminal violation, they have the power to arrest the suspects and seize the evidence. When the suspects are brought to trial, agents are expected to assist in preparing the prosecution's case, including but not limited to appearing on the witness stand.

#### *Qualifications*

Applicants must be U.S. citizens between the ages of 21 and 37 at the time of appointment, although the upper age limitation may be waived for those who hold, or have held in the past, a federal law enforcement position. You will need to pass a personal interview, a physical exam (including vision and hearing tests), and a background investigation. A bachelor's degree, three years of work experience, or an equivalent combination of education and work experience are also required.

#### *Training*

New recruits are sent to an 18-week training program at the Federal Law Enforcement Training Center in Glynco, Georgia. Coursework includes immigration and naturalization laws and investigative techniques, in addition to other relevant subjects.

#### *Finding a Job*

To apply, you need to establish an eligibility rating with the OPM, either by taking a written test or completing a questionnaire describing your previous experience. Contact the INS for details at www.ins.usdoj.gov.

### INS Immigration Inspectors

This position is responsible for permitting the entry of eligible persons into the country, while preventing the entry of those who aren't allowed on U.S. soil. Immigration inspector is a uniformed position. They are stationed at land ports, seaports, airports, and any other points of entry where travelers arrive from other countries. Immigration inspectors process literally millions of people each year from these locations, examining passports, visas, and other legal documentation. They are expected to known all current laws, regulations, policies, and court and administrative decisions that govern legal entry into the United States.

### *Qualifications*

To apply for this position, you must:

- be a U.S. citizen
- pass a personal interview
- pass a physical examination (including vision and hearing tests)
- pass a background investigation
- have either a bachelor's degree or at least three years of responsible work experience

There are no minimum or maximum age limits for becoming an INS immigration inspector.

### *Training*

New hires participate in a 14-week training program at the Federal Law Enforcement Training Center in Glynco, Georgia. The program includes courses in Spanish, nationality laws, and firearms proficiency.

### *Finding a Job*

For information on testing and application procedures, you should contact the OPM, the INS (www.ins.usdoj.gov), or the nearest INS regional office (listed on page 105).

**JUST THE FACTS**

The Office of Community Oriented Policing Services (COPS) was added to the Department of Justice by Attorney General Janet Reno. It is responsible for adding 100,000 new officers to local police agencies and for promoting community policing strategies. In 1995, COPS was appropriated $1.3 billion. Five years later, it had already hired almost 60,000 new officers and sheriff's deputies.

## Federal Bureau of Investigation (FBI)

The Mission of the FBI is to uphold the law through the investigation of violations of federal criminal law; to protect the United States from foreign intelligence and terrorist activities; to provide leadership and law enforcement assistance to federal, state, local, and international agencies; and to perform these responsibilities in a manner that is responsive to the needs of the public and is faithful to the Constitution of the United States.

— FBI MISSION STATEMENT

The FBI is well known through its many portrayals in the media. Hundreds of television programs, feature films, and books have explored this main investigative arm of the U.S. Department of Justice. This high visibility is partly responsible for the large number of applicants to the FBI, meaning there is strong competition for positions. The qualifications are among the strictest in federal agencies, and the job itself is demanding. Special Agent Damon Katz notes:

> Managing a heavy caseload is the hardest part of my job. Some cases are simple, some are complex, but they all require organization and attention to the details. Juggling the fieldwork and the paperwork of 10 or 20 cases at once is challenging.

The FBI has responsibility for foreign counterintelligence matters, conducting background investigations on nominees for top jobs in the United States government, and for criminal investigations that often cause headlines across the world (the World Trade Center bombing, for example). They have jurisdiction in more than 200 types of criminal cases, including bank robberies, espionage, terrorism, civil rights violations, fraud, and assassination attempts on federal officials.

### Special Agent

Special agents work on high-security cases and have the FBI's sophisticated resources at their disposal; however, their basic duties are the same as other law enforcement investigators. They search for facts and evidence that can be used to solve criminal cases; handle masses of paperwork; conduct undercover surveillance operations; question informants, witnesses, and suspects; and arrest suspects. As a case concludes, agents write detailed reports.

The information and evidence they collect is submitted to the appropriate U.S. attorney or Department of Justice official for legal action, if warranted. If the case goes to trial, the agent testifies in court when called.

The FBI divides its investigations into seven programs:

- Applicant Matters
- Civil Rights
- Counterterrorism
- Financial Crime
- Foreign Counterintelligence
- Organized Crime/Drugs
- Violent Crimes and Major Offenders

The FBI does not go through the OPM when they hire for special agent positions. Because of the FBI's diverse responsibilities, they have been given more latitude in personnel matters than most other federal agencies. Everyone who goes to work for the FBI is considered to be in the "excepted service"—which means FBI employees are not civil service employees. Therefore, the Director of the FBI can make personnel decisions relating to hiring, applicant qualifications, promotions, and discipline that wouldn't be made if the agency operated under civil service regulations.

#### *Qualifications*

To be considered by the FBI, you must be a U.S. citizen between the ages of 23 and 37 upon appointment. You must have a bachelor's degree from an accredited four-year college or university and you must have three years of full-time work experience. If you are a law school graduate or hold another graduate degree in a field for which the FBI has a need, then they may waive the three-year work requirement.

The FBI gives a series of written tests that are computer-scored at FBI headquarters in Washington, D.C. These are followed by a formal interview, and then an intense background investigation. Special agents in charge of background investigations interview neighbors, work associates, personal references, past employers, and family members, as well as verify all the information listed on prospective agents' applications.

Agents must pass a drug test and a polygraph examination. A physical examination may also be required. FBI personnel go over the results of a background investigation and assess it for a final hiring decision.

The FBI has five entrance programs under which you may qualify to be hired as a special agent. These programs consider your education and work experience based on one of these five possibilities:

1. *Law*—graduates of an American Bar Association (ABA)-accredited law school who have two years of resident undergraduate work
2. *Accounting*—graduates of an accredited four-year college or university with a degree in accounting
3. *Language*—graduates of an accredited four-year college or university who are fluent in a foreign language for which the FBI has a current need
4. *Diversified*—graduates of an accredited four-year college or university who have at least three years of full-time work experience
5. *Engineering/Science*—graduates of an accredited college or university who have either a master's or other advanced degree in engineering or computer science or a bachelor's degree in engineering or computer science and at least three years of work experience

### *Training*

Newly appointed special agents undergo 15 weeks of extensive training at the FBI Academy in Quantico, Virginia. Classroom instruction includes a wide range of academic and investigative topics, as well as physical fitness, firearms training, and defensive tactics. Before graduation, there is training in investigative, intelligence gathering, interview, and interrogation techniques.

### *Finding a Job*

To apply for a position with the FBI, contact the field office nearest to you. A list of those offices may be found in Appendix B. Also check the FBI's website at www.fbi.gov.

## Drug Enforcement Administration (DEA)

The DEA is charged with a mission to enforce U.S. laws on illegal drug trafficking and their efforts to prevent drug abuse. In this effort, the over 4,000 agents are skilled in the use of the latest, most sophisticated investigative tools. Because of the high-profile nature of the DEA's work, they demand much from their recruits, and both the academic and physical training requirements are strenuous.

After hiring and training by the DEA, special agents and investigators track down major suppliers of narcotics and other dangerous drugs in both the United States and abroad. Their focus is on the distribution of illicit drugs such as heroin, cocaine, hallucinogens, and marijuana, as well as both illegal and legal trade in depressants, stimulants, and other controlled substances.

### Special Agent

DEA special agents' duties are to uncover criminal drug activities and catch violators of federal drug laws so that they can be prosecuted. Because the DEA focuses primarily on large-scale illegal drug operations, the work is dangerous. Agents are involved in planning and conducting investigations that target individuals and organizations who make and distribute illegal drugs and narcotics and those who divert legal controlled substances for unlawful purposes. Surveillance and undercover work play big roles in this job.

DEA special agents collect information by following paper trails; questioning informants, witnesses, and suspects; and using top-notch investigative skills. After they round up sufficient evidence and have probable cause, they arrest suspects and confiscate illegal drug supplies. Courts across the country rely on the results of agents' investigations and their testimony to get convictions.

Some of their time may be spent passing on knowledge of drug control and drug-related crime to other law enforcement professionals, communities, and organizations nationwide. Agents are also expected to work with other federal, state, and local law enforcement agencies. And they work with foreign governments, agencies, and law enforcement to help develop intelligence networks and investigate unlawful drug trade.

DEA special agents must be willing to accept assignments anywhere in the United States upon appointment. Foreign assignments are also possible. Relocation may be necessary at any stage in an agent's career. The DEA even has its agents sign a statement agreeing to this condition before offering employment.

### *Qualifications*

You must be a U.S. citizen between 21 and 37 years of age at the time of appointment, and you must possess a valid driver's license. You must also be in excellent physical condition, possess sharp hearing acuity, and have uncorrected vision of at least 20/200. If corrected, your vision can be 20/20 in one eye and 20/40 in the other. The DEA disqualifies anyone who has had radial keratotomy (RK) surgery to correct vision problems.

The DEA requires a college degree from an accredited college or university; it doesn't matter in what field of study. In addition, you'll need either one year of work experience or an overall GPA of 2.5 on a 4.0 scale and a GPA of 3.5 in your major field of study, with an academic standing in the upper one-third of a graduating class or major subdivision; membership in a scholastic honor society; and one year of graduate study.

You must also pass the special agent interview process and successfully complete a polygraph examination, a psychological examination, and an intense background investigation. Drug screening is a part of the process, and once you are hired, you will be subject to random testing throughout your career.

### *Training*

All DEA special agent trainees participate in a 16-week DEA training program conducted at the FBI Academy in Quantico, Virginia. This course includes instruction in drug laws, drug identification, investigative techniques, arrest, search and seizure, ethics, self-defense, use of firearms, court procedures, and criminology. To earn a DEA badge, you must pass this course of instruction, as well as a physical fitness test. New agents are required to complete a probationary/trial period of three to four years after successfully completing the basic training course.

### *Finding a Job*

More information is available about the DEA on their website at www.usdoj.gov/dea. Or call 1-800-DEA-4288 or write to:

Drug Enforcement Administration
Office of Personnel
1405 I Street N.W.
Washington, D.C. 20537

Applications should be sent to the nearest regional DEA office (listed below) for hiring consideration. You'll need to provide specific forms and documents with your application. This may include a resume or Optional Application for Federal Employment, a Background Survey Questionnaire (OPM Form 1386), and a college transcript.

## Regional DEA Offices

### PHOENIX DIVISION

3010 North 2nd Street
Suite 301
Phoenix, AZ 85012
(602) 664-5600

### LOS ANGELES DIVISION

255 East Temple Street, 20th floor
Los Angeles, CA 90012
(213) 894-4258

### SAN DIEGO DIVISION

402 West 35th Street
National City, CA 91950
(619) 585-4241

### SAN FRANCISCO DIVISION

450 Golden Gate Avenue, Room 12215
San Francisco, CA 94102
(415) 436-7900

**ROCKY MOUNTAIN DIVISION**
115 Inverness Drive
East Englewood, CO 80112
(303) 705-7300

**WASHINGTON D.C. DIVISION**
400 Sixth Street SW, Room 2558
Washington, DC 20024
(202) 401-7512

**MIAMI DIVISION**
8400 NW 53rd Street
Miami, FL 33166
(305) 590-4812

**ATLANTA DIVISION**
75 Spring Street SW, Room 740
Atlanta, GA 30303
(404) 331-4401

**CHICAGO DIVISION**
230 South Dearborn Street, Suite 1200
Chicago, IL 60604
(312) 353-7875

## Bureau of Prisons

The Bureau of Prisons (BOP) is the second largest employer in the law enforcement field at the federal level. The BOP is responsible for hiring all corrections officers who work at federal prison institutions nationwide. These institutions are for people who have either violated federal laws or are awaiting trial for violating federal laws.

The need for federal corrections officers to staff new institutions, combined with a high turnover rate, makes the BOP one of the best federal employment opportunities. However, they still have more competitive requirements for their corrections officers than most state or county correctional facilities.

### Qualifications

As you've seen in the general description of duties outlined in Chapter 4 of this book, corrections is a challenging field. To be hired by the BOP, you must:

- be between the ages of 21 and 37
- have vision that is 20/20 corrected (20/70 uncorrected)
- have a four-year college degree, or
- have a minimum of three years of previous experience in law enforcement, corrections, or an area of general experience such as teaching, counseling, or parole/probation worker

### Training

All federal corrections officers attend a 13-day, 120-hour training program at the federal training facility in Glynco, Georgia. Training classes start at 7:30 A.M. and end at 4:30 P.M. Classroom topics include legal issues, communication, self-defense training, and firearms proficiency.

After the training program, you report for work at the facility that hired you. That facility will continue your training, teaching their policies and procedures. For one year you will be under probation and closely monitored by a supervisor.

### Finding a Job

To begin the process, you must fill out the OPM application form 1203AW Form C for the BOP. You can get this application online at www.bop.gov, or by calling or writing to:

Federal Bureau of Prisons
National Recruitment Office
Room 460
Washington, DC 20534
(202) 307-1490

Another way to get an application is to request one from the personnel office of any federal prison facility. You may also get an application by calling or writing to any regional BOP office. The regional BOP offices are located at:

### MID-ATLANTIC REGIONAL OFFICE

1101 Junction Drive
Suite 100-N
Annapolis Junction, MD 20701
(301) 317-3100
Fax: (301) 317-3115

### NORTH CENTRAL REGIONAL OFFICE

Gateway Complex Tower 11, 8th floor
400 State Avenue
Kansas City, KS 66101
(913) 621-3939
Fax: (913) 551-1175

### NORTHEAST REGIONAL OFFICE

U.S. Customs House, 7th floor
2nd and Chestnut Streets
Philadelphia, PA 19106
(215) 597-6317
Fax: (215) 521-7476

### SOUTH CENTRAL REGIONAL OFFICE

4211 Cedar Springs Road, Suite 300
Dallas, TX 75219
(214) 767-9700
Fax: (214) 224-3420

### SOUTHEAST REGIONAL OFFICE

3800 Camp Creek Parkway SW, Building 2000
Atlanta, GA 30331
(678) 686-1200
Fax: (678) 686-1229

**WESTERN REGIONAL OFFICE**

7950 Dublin Boulevard, 3rd floor
Dublin, CA 94568
(925) 803-4700
Fax: (925) 803-4802

## Marshals Service

The U.S. Marshals Service is probably best known for its Witness Protection Program, created in the 1970s. But it is also involved with nearly every facet of the federal justice system. As the country's oldest federal law enforcement agency (established in 1789), it employs over 4,000 officers. Deputy U.S. marshals provide security in the federal courts as well as investigative and security services related to federal prisoners and fugitives. They apprehend fugitives and transport prisoners. Marshals also sell property seized from criminals and restore order during riots and other violent situations. Their Special Operations Group is involved in crises such as civil disturbances and terrorist incidents. Finally, they safeguard witnesses who testify against organized crime activities in federal and state court cases through the Witness Protection Program.

**IN THE NEWS**

The U.S. Marshals Service was the first federal law enforcement agency to be accredited by the Commission on Accreditation for Law Enforcement Agencies (CALEA). It received this honor in June of 2000, after meeting the professional standards set by CALEA. The standards, which number over 400, are designed to increase the accountability of personnel at all levels. Attorney General Janet Reno accepted the award for the Marshals Service.

### Deputy U.S. Marshal

Deputy U.S. marshals answer to U.S. marshals, who are appointed by the president to head the 94 judicial districts across the country and in Guam and Puerto Rico. Deputies are officers of the federal court, and they coordinate security operations during federal court cases; this means protecting federal judges, attorneys, and other court officials and participants. They also make sure that proper security systems and personnel are in place throughout federal court buildings. A deputy marshal's role is similar to that of a bailiff during state and local trials: maintaining order in the courtroom, restraining violent persons, conducting weapons searches, and serving as guards and escorts.

Deputy U.S. marshals also serve court orders, such as subpoenas or criminal warrants; seize and manage property from criminal activities; and maintain custody of federal prisoners. Those assigned to the Witness Protection Program are responsible for the safety and well-being of federal witnesses against organized crime.

As a law enforcement agent of the attorney general, U.S. Department of Justice, tracking federal fugitives is one of a Marshal's most important responsibilities. (A federal fugitive is someone who has either escaped from custody, violated parole or probation guidelines, or failed to obey orders to appear in federal court.) This work often involves travel and relocation. Deputy marshals may also be asked to help foreign countries by locating their fugitives who have escaped to the United States.

Within the U.S. Marshals Service is the highly selective unit called the Special Operations Group (SOG). The SOG is called out to help with national emergencies in any U.S. judicial district; members are on call 24 hours a day and can be assembled within hours to intervene in situations such as large-scale public riots or a crisis triggered by terrorism. The SOG is a voluntary unit, but membership is restricted to the most qualified, skilled, and physically fit. Members are chosen after they go through specialized training.

#### *Qualifications*

To qualify for a deputy U.S. marshal position, you must be a U.S. citizen between the ages of 21 and 37 at the time of appointment. You will need to pass a written test, which is administered by the OPM, as well as a personal interview, a physical exam (including vision, hearing, and physical performance tests), and a background investigation. Minimum education/experience requirements can be satisfied with either a bachelor's degree from an accredited college or university and three years of responsible work experience or an equivalent combination of education and work experience. (One academic year of full-time undergraduate study is considered equivalent to nine months of work experience.)

### *Training*

You will be asked to complete a 16-week basic training program at the Federal Law Enforcement Training Center in Glynco, Georgia. The program consists of an eight-week criminal investigator's course and five weeks of courses related to the specific duties of a deputy U.S. marshal.

### *Finding a Job*

Testing information is available from the OPM or directly from the U.S. Marshals Service:

Employment and Compensation Division
Field Staffing Branch
600 Army/Navy Drive
Arlington, VA 22202-4210
(202) 307-9100

Check out their website at www.usdoj.gov/marshals for additional information.

## U.S. TREASURY DEPARTMENT

The U.S. Treasury Department's major duties include formulating economic, fiscal, and tax policies; enforcing federal laws; protecting the President and other officials; and overseeing the manufacturing of currency. The law enforcement arm of the U.S. Treasury Department includes some well-known agencies: the Customs Service, the Secret Service, and the Bureau of Alcohol, Tobacco, and Firearms (ATF).

## U.S. Customs Service

This agency, established in 1789 by the first Congress of the United States, is charged with regulating and enforcing federal patent, trademark, and copyright laws, specifically by monitoring ports of entry into the country. All law enforcement officials employed by the U.S. Customs Services have duties that in one way or another support this overall mission. This includes efforts to prevent and intercept persons engaged in criminal acts such as illegal smuggling of merchandise and goods, revenue fraud on imported or exported goods, drug and arms trafficking, and cargo thefts.

### Customs Special Agent

The job of a customs special agent resembles that of a police detective, although special agents operate under a much wider scope of authority and territory. The cases they investigate fall under two related categories: stopping and prosecuting illegal imports and exports, and collecting revenue (tariff duties and taxes) owed to the government on legal imports and exports.

What they do on a day-to-day basis depends on the case to which they are assigned. If the case involves the collection of evidence and information, agents may either investigate public and private records or question suspects, witnesses, or other sources to get information. Setting up complex surveillances and undercover operations are also part of the job.

Special agents also search ships, aircraft, and land vehicles. They seize smuggled goods and illegal shipments of narcotics, arms, and other contraband, as well as detain vehicles or vessels used to transport illegal or suspect goods. They have the authority to arrest persons connected with acts that violate federal laws governed by the U.S. Customs Service.

### IN THE NEWS

An undercover website operated by U.S. Customs agents caught "cyberpirates" buying and reselling counterfeit "smart cards," which provided free access to satellite television service. The 22-month investigation, called Operation Smartcard.Net, involved customs agents selling over 3,000 illegal cards to dealers and almost 400 to individuals. It is a felony to distribute devices that assist in the unauthorized decoding of satellite programming; there is a maximum penalty of five years in prison and a $500,000 fine.

There are a wide range of cases to handle as a special agent: drug trafficking by organized crime syndicates, tax evasion by international businesses that falsify the value of otherwise legal shipments, and individuals failing to declare purchases made while visiting other countries. Whatever the case, an important part of the job is to keep accurate records of investigations so that criminal charges can be made and supported. And special agents are frequent visitors to the courtroom witness stand and assets to the prosecutors who take their cases to trial.

### *Qualifications*

To qualify for a customs agent position, you must be a U.S. citizen of at least 21 but under 37 years of age. You will need to take the Treasury Enforcement Agent (TEA) written examination, which is designed to gauge basic skills needed for investigative work, such as good judgment, logic, planning, and communication skills. You must pass the TEA, a physical examination (including vision and hearing tests), a background investigation, and a drug screening. In addition, you must have either a bachelor's degree from an accredited college in any field of study, or at least one year of general work experience and two years of related (law enforcement) experience.

### *Training*

Once accepted as a special agent recruit, you will participate in a 14-week training program at the Federal Law Enforcement Training Center in Glynco, Georgia. The program includes written tests, physical performance tests, and graded practical exercises. Areas covered by this training include the use of firearms, undercover and surveillance techniques, rules of evidence and courtroom procedures, customs laws and regulations, and various methods of investigation and law enforcement.

### *Finding a Job*

The TEA examination is administered by the OPM. More information on testing and application information is available from www.customs.ustreas.gov or:

U.S. Customs Service
Office of Human Resources
Enforcement Division
P.O. Box 7108
Washington, D.C. 20044

### Customs Inspector

Customs inspectors track violations in federal customs and commerce laws. They are responsible for inspecting not only the personal baggage of travelers entering or leaving the United States, but also large cargo transported by vehicles on land, air, and sea. In all cases, customs inspectors are trained to know what to look for and how to handle situations where laws have been violated.

This is not strictly an office job. In order to regulate commercial shipments, customs inspectors are authorized to board and examine aircraft, ships, trains, and other vehicles of transport. Part of their job may be to examine cargo documentation as well as the actual cargo to ensure that no smuggling, fraud, or theft takes place. On a ship, for example, they may oversee the unloading of cargo containers, question crew and passengers, and conduct physical searches if any criminal activity is suspected. These efforts are aimed at uncovering the transport of illegal goods—such as narcotics or weaponry—plus goods that have been undervalued, have not been reported, or that exceed legal limits of the amount allowed in or out of the country.

The work of customs inspectors is to make sure duty fees are properly assessed and collected on items brought into the country. They have the authority to inspect baggage and search passengers to reveal whether undeclared goods are being carried or illegal goods are being smuggled. Inspectors can also detain and question passengers to determine whether intentional fraud was committed. If so, they seize items as evidence and report the incident for legal action by the U.S. Customs Service. When the situation warrants, they are empowered to place individuals under arrest for later criminal prosecution.

#### *Qualifications*

In addition to being a U.S. citizen, you must pass a physical examination, a background investigation, and a drug test. You will need to have either a bachelor's degree from an accredited college or at least three years of responsible work experience. A written test—the Customs Inspector Examination—is also administered to applicants for this position. However, by meeting certain educational standards you may be eligible for an Outstanding Scholar Program. Specifically, you must have graduated from college with either a GPA of at least 3.4 on a 4.0 scale or have been in the upper 10% of your graduating class. If you meet either of these standards, the written test may be waived.

#### *Training*

As a customs inspector recruit, you will participate in an 11-week training program at the Federal Law Enforcement Training Center in Glynco, Georgia. This training includes a series of written and physical tests as well as graded practical exercises (such as firearms proficiency).

#### *Finding a Job*

The Customs Service administers the Customs Inspector Examination. More information on testing and application procedures is available at www.customs.ustreas.gov, or through:

U.S. Customs Service
Office of Human Resources
Operations Division
P.O. Box 14156
Washington, D.C. 20044

Three other law enforcement positions are available through the U.S. Customs Service to serve the overall goals of this agency: canine enforcement officer; customs pilot; and import specialist. They each have duties that bring them together regularly with special agents and customs inspectors to investigate customs-related violations. The job qualifications differ in some significant ways, however. These positions are highly specialized and require certain technical expertise or aptitude in particular areas.

### Customs Canine Enforcement Officer

These officers are responsible for training and handling dogs to uncover the smuggling of illegal narcotics and dangerous drugs, including marijuana, cocaine, heroin, and other controlled substances. They are assigned to ports of entry across the United States, and play a vital role in searching suspect persons and property. Canine enforcement officers are often called in to assist with formal investigations, such as those conducted by customs special agents, leading to the apprehension and arrest of smugglers.

#### *Qualifications*

To qualify for this position, you must be a U.S. citizen; pass a physical examination, background investigation, and drug screening; and have at least three years of responsible work experience or a bachelor's degree from an accredited college. You will not need to take a written test. Related experience, especially any that demonstrates an affinity for dogs, is an obvious plus.

#### *Training*

Recruits participate in 15 weeks of enforcement and dog handler training at the U.S. Customs Service Canine Enforcement Training Center in Front Royal, Virginia. This training includes written and physical tests as well as graded practical exercises, including one on firearms proficiency.

#### *Finding a Job*

Recruitment bulletins are issued by the OPM when the U.S. Customs Service has openings for this position. More information on testing and application procedures is available at www.customs.ustreas.gov, or through:

U.S. Customs Service
Office of Human Resources
Operations Division
P.O. Box 14060
Washington, D.C. 20044

### Customs Pilot

Customs pilots are licensed, experienced pilots who conduct air surveillance to detect customs violations using a specially equipped fleet of planes and helicopters, which are maintained by the Customs Service. Flight duties could involve identifying illegal traffic on the U.S. borders between Mexico and Canada, or pursuing smugglers by air along coastal areas. Customs pilots are also authorized to detain and question suspects, conduct physical searches, and make arrests.

#### *Qualifications*

This position has strict technical requirements, which include holding a current Federal Aviation Agency (FAA) commercial pilot's license and passing a current FAA Class I physical examination. In addition, you must be a U.S. citizen of at least 21 but under 37 years of age, and pass a background investigation and a drug screening. The U.S. Customs Service will determine your eligibility based on your application and your Record of Aeronautical Experience (Form OPM-1170-21).

#### *Training*

Recruits participate in a 16-week training program at the Federal Law Enforcement Training Center in Glynco, Georgia. This training includes written and physical tests as well as graded practical exercises, including one on firearms proficiency.

#### *Finding a Job*

More information on testing and application procedures is available through:

U.S. Customs Service
Office of Human Resources
Delegated Examining Unit/Pilots
P.O. Box 14060
Washington, D.C. 20044

### Customs Import Specialists

These specialists perform a variety of administrative and investigative functions, primarily related to revenue collection on imported goods. The word "specialist" in this title indicates skill in appraising the value of commercial imports and calculating payments owed the government on such shipments. If you are hired in this capacity, you'll work with other customs officials and you may request to assist in formal investigations into illegally suspect shipments, incidents of fraud, and schemes aimed at dodging tariff and trade laws.

### *Qualifications*

Requirements for this position include being a U.S. citizen of at least 21 but under 37 years of age and passing a physical examination, a background investigation, and a drug screening. You also must have at least three years of progressively responsible work experience or equivalent education (one academic year of full-time undergraduate study equals nine months of work experience). To help gauge your own interest in this position, keep in mind that enforcing the law in this case means having an aptitude for math, economics, paperwork, and understanding complex trade regulations.

A written test is required before you can take on this position. The ACWA (Administrative Careers with America) Examination for Law Enforcement and Investigative Positions is administered by the OPM. You will need to submit an Admission Notice and Record Card (Form 5000-B) to the OPM location where you want to take the test. The OPM will return the admission notice to you to tell you when and where to report for the test.

### *Training*

Recruits participate in six weeks of technical training at the Federal Law Enforcement Training Center in Glynco, Georgia. This training includes a series of written and graded practical exercises.

### *Finding a Job*

More information on testing and application procedures is available on www.customs.ustreas.gov, or through:

U.S. Customs Service
Office of Human Resources
Operations Division
P.O. Box 14156
Washington, D.C. 20044

## U.S. Secret Service

The most visible responsibility of this organization is the protection of the U.S. President, Vice President, their families, and other government officials. Special agents of the Secret Service handle security operations when these officials are traveling. Officers in a special unit—the U.S. Secret Service Uniformed division—provide security at the White House, at the official residence of the Vice President, and foreign diplomatic missions (primarily in the Washington, D.C. area).

When the Secret Service was founded in 1865, its mission was to investigate the counterfeiting of U.S. currency, and to uncover other forms of currency fraud. This is still a part of their job, but with new technology, its scope has been expanded to include credit and debit card fraud as well as computer fraud.

The U.S. Secret Service has over 4,500 agents assigned to its different divisions. It maintains over 152 district offices in the United States and abroad.

### U.S. Secret Service District Offices:

Albany, GA
Albany, NY
Albuquerque, NM
Anchorage, AK
Annapolis, MD
Atlanta, GA
Atlantic City, NJ
Austin, TX
Baltimore, MD
Baton Rouge, LA
Birmingham, AL
Boise, ID
Boston, MA
Buffalo, NY
Charleston, SC
Charleston, WV
Charlotte, NC
Chattanooga, TN
Cheyenne, WY
Chicago, IL
Cincinnati, OH
Cleveland, OH
Colorado Springs, CO
Columbus, OH
Columbia, SC
Concord, NH
Dallas, TX
Dayton, OH
Denver, CO
Des Moines, IA
Detroit, MI
El Paso, TX

Evansville, IN
Fresno, CA
Grand Rapids, MI
Great Falls, MT
Greensboro, NC
Greenville, SC
Honolulu, HI
Houston, TX
Indianapolis, IN
Jackson, MS
Jacksonville, FL
Jamaica, NY
Kansas City, MO
Knoxville, TN
Las Vegas, NV
Laurel, MD
Lexington, KY
Little Rock, AR
Los Angeles, CA
Louisville, KY
Lubbock, TX
Madison, WI
McAllen, TX
Melville, NY
Memphis, TN
Miami, FL
Milwaukee, WI
Minneapolis, MN
Mobile, AL
Montgomery, AL
Nashville, TN
Newark, NJ
New Haven, CT
New Orleans, LA
New York, NY
Norfolk, VA
Oklahoma City, OK
Omaha, NE
Orlando, FL
Philadelphia, PA
Phoenix, AZ
Pittsburgh, PA
Portland, ME
Portland, OR
Providence, RI
Raleigh, NC
Reno, NV
Richmond, VA
Rochester, NY
Riverside, CA
Roanoke, VA
Sacramento, CA
Saginaw, MI
Salt Lake City, UT
San Antonio, TX
San Diego, CA
San Francisco, CA
San Jose, CA
Santa Ana, CA
Savannah, GA
Scranton, PA
Seattle, WA
Shreveport, LA
Sioux Falls, SD
South Bend, IN
Spokane, WA
Springfield, IL
Springfield, MO
St. Louis, MO
Syracuse, NY
Tallahassee, FL
Tampa, FL

Toledo, OH
Trenton, NJ
Tucson, AZ
Tulsa, OK
Tyler, TX
Ventura, CA
Washington, DC
West Palm Beach, FL
White Plains, NY
Wilmington, DE
Witchita, KS
Wilmington, DE

## Overseas Offices:

Bangkok, Thailand
Berlin, Germany
Bogota, Columbia
Bonn, Germany
Hong Kong, China
Manila, Philippines
Milan, Italy
Montreal, Canada
Moscow, Russia
Nicosia, Cyprus
Ottawa, Canada
Paris, France
San Juan, Puerto Rico
Rome, Italy

### Special Agent

These agents are charged with the duty of protecting:

- the President, Vice President, President-elect, Vice President-elect, and their immediate families
- former Presidents, their spouses or widows (until remarriage), and their minor children (up to age 16)
- major presidential and vice presidential candidates within 120 days of a general presidential election
- visiting heads of foreign states or governments

They may also be assigned by the President to guard other foreign dignitaries visiting the United States, or official representatives of the United States while they are on missions abroad.

A significant part of their protective duties involve making sure that all necessary security measures are in place for public appearances. An advance team of special agents will scope out locations to determine methods of transportation, travel routes, the type of personnel and security equipment needed, and alternate routes and facilities to be used in case of an emergency. They are expected to make use of highly sophisticated communications and surveillance equipment to carry out assignments. Special agents also rely upon other federal, state, and local law enforcement agencies for help with anything from background information to equipment and personnel.

In addition to their protective duties, Secret Service agents are also charged with the investigation of currency fraud. This includes counterfeiting operations; the forgery or theft of U.S. government checks, bonds, and securities; and credit card, computer, and electronic transfer fraud. If assigned to a fraud case, agents gather background data and evidence; arrange for surveillance and/or undercover work; question informants, witnesses, and suspects; arrest suspects; and seize evidence. When the charged are brought to trial, special agents' reports and testimony will help the U.S. attorneys to make their case.

### *Qualifications*

Before you can be hired as a special agent you must be a U.S. citizen of at least 21 but under 37 years of age at the time of appointment, and you must pass the following:

- the TEA written examination
- a personal interview
- a polygraph exam
- a background investigation
- a medical exam (including vision and hearing tests)

A bachelor's degree from an accredited college or university in any field of study is also required. You may be able to qualify instead with at least three years of work experience, two of those in criminal investigative work, or with the equivalent in relevant work experience and education. As with many other federal law enforcement positions, frequent travel and the possibility of relocation are to be expected.

#### *Training*

Special agent recruits receive general investigative training at the Federal Law Enforcement Training Center in Glynco, Georgia. They also receive specialized instruction at the Secret Service training facilities near Washington, D.C. This course of training includes protective techniques, criminal law, the use of firearms, defensive measures, surveillance techniques, and undercover operations.

#### *Finding a Job*

To apply and sign up to take the Treasury Enforcement Agent (TEA) Examination, contact the nearest OPM or Secret Service field office. Information is available on their website at www.treas.gov/usss, including application forms you can download and fill out. You can also call 1-202-406-5800, or write to:

U.S. Secret Service Personnel Division
950 H Street, N.W.
Washington, D.C. 20001

### Uniformed Division Officer

These officers are more visible than Secret Service agents. They perform high-level security and law enforcement functions and are assigned to the Washington, D.C. metropolitan area to cover security for:

- the White House grounds and any buildings which house presidential offices
- the official residence of the Vice President
- foreign diplomatic missions or embassies located in the District of Columbia (or other regions under special order of the President)

The uniformed division operates much like a police force, constantly on the watch for any disturbances, suspicious situations, and criminal activity.

As an officer, your job will be to make sure all the necessary security systems and equipment are in place. You'll also conduct regular patrols to monitor the grounds, buildings, and security equipment in your assigned area. Officers are assigned to fixed security posts at entrance and exit points to ensure that visitors are authorized to be on the premises. You'll have the authority to question, search, and arrest trespassers or others involved in illegal or disruptive activities.

### *Qualifications*

To qualify for the uniformed division, you must be a U.S. citizen of at least 21 but under 37 years of age at the time of appointment. Once you have passed a written exam, you'll go through a personal interview. You must also pass a background investigation, a polygraph test, and a medical examination (including vision and hearing tests.) A high school diploma or GED satisfies the minimum educational requirements.

### *Training*

Uniformed division officer recruits are trained at the Federal Law Enforcement Training Center in Glynco, Georgia and receive specialized instruction at the Secret Service training facilities near Washington, D.C. This training includes courses in police procedures, psychology, police-community relations, criminal law, first aid, laws of arrest, search and seizure, use of firearms, and defensive tactics.

### *Finding a Job*

Tests and interviews are conducted by the U.S. Secret Service. The written exam is usually given on a quarterly basis in the Washington, D.C. area and periodically in other major U.S. cities. For more information, visit their website at www.ustreas.gov/usss. You can also call 1-800-827-7783, or write to:

U.S. Secret Service
Attn: Uniformed Division Recruiter
1800 G Street, N.W.
Washington, D.C. 20223

## Bureau of Alcohol, Tobacco, and Firearms (ATF)

The over 2,000 agents of the ATF are charged with investigating the criminal use of firearms and explosives and enforcing federal alcohol and tobacco regulations. Their mission is to:

- reduce violent crime through enforcement of firearms laws
- protect the public by regulating handling and storage of explosives and criminal misuse of explosives
- collect revenue from legal trade within the alcohol, tobacco, and firearms industries
- enforce and administer the Federal Alcohol Administration Act
- help states to stop the sale and distribution of contraband cigarettes

### Special Agent

Like most federal agencies, the ATF works closely with other federal, state, and local law enforcement agencies. ATF special agents help these agencies in the fight against crime by investigating violations of federal laws relating to explosives, arson, firearms, liquor, and tobacco. This work puts them in contact with some of the most dangerous criminals and criminal activities in the world, including terrorist bombings and the trafficking of weapons and ammunition. Agents are trained to:

- set up surveillance operations
- work undercover
- participate in raids
- obtain search warrants
- make arrests
- interview suspects and witnesses
- search for physical evidence

Special agents also review evidence at the conclusion of an investigation and prepare a case report if evidence so justifies, as well as assist the U.S attorney in the preparation and presentation of the case before and during a trial. After the arrests are made and the reports written, special agents help prepare cases for criminal prosecution and give court testimony when called to the witness stand.

The ATF runs a Gang Resistance Education and Training (GREAT) program in middle schools across the country. This prevention strategy is taught by full-time, sworn police officers after they receive 80 hours of training from the ATF. Police Departments can recommend their officers, who must have a minimum of three years of experience, and meet other requirements to be accepted. For more information on the GREAT program, call 1-800-726-7070, or write to them at great@atfhq.atf.treas.gov.

### Qualifications

ATF special agents must be U.S. citizens of at least 21 but under 37 years of age at the time of appointment. A four-year degree from an accredited college or university is required. In some cases, the equivalent in work experience, or education plus work experience, may be considered instead.

Vision must be within acceptable levels: distance vision without correction must be at least 20/100 in each eye, correctable to 20/30 in one eye and 20/20 in the other. Applicants must pass an exhaustive background investigation, a medical examination, and a drug screening; weight must be in good proportion to height. Because of the strenuous physical requirements of the job, agents must also show that they have the strength and stamina to perform their future duties.

### Training

Special agent trainees receive eight weeks of training in general law enforcement and investigative techniques at the Federal Law Enforcement Training Center in Glynco, Georgia. This training includes courses in surveillance techniques, rules of evidence, undercover assignments, arrest and raid techniques, and the use of firearms. Later, they get "new agent training," covering the specific duties of ATF special agents, such as instruction related to laws enforced by the ATF Bureau, case report writing, firearms and explosives operations, bomb scene searches, and arson investigations.

### *Finding a Job*

The ATF does not keep a list of qualified applicants. If you want to be considered for a position, you must watch for a specific job vacancy announcement number. You can find these announcements on their website, www.atf.treas.gov, or at the OPM website, www.opm.gov. When you get the announcement number, contact the OPM for the proper paperwork. All of the announcements will have a job description, qualifications for the job, deadlines for application submission, and application procedures. Check the beginning of this chapter for instructions on getting what you need from the OPM.

The most highly qualified candidates become eligible to take the written Treasury Enforcement Agent (TEA) examination through the OPM. To find out when it is being given, call the nearest regional office (listed in the box below). After passing the exam, your name is added to a roster of eligible candidates ranked by test score results. The names of the top four or five candidates are sent to the ATF by the OPM. The ATF then continues the application process.

**ATF Regional Offices:**

Atlanta, GA, Field Division: 404-679-5170

Baltimore, MD, Field Division: 410-962-0897

Boston, MA, Field Division: 617-565-7042

Charlotte, NC, Field Division: 704-716-1800

Chicago, IL, Field Division: 312-353-6935

Columbus, OH, Field Division: 614-469-5303

Dallas, TX, Field Division: 214-767-2250

Detroit, MI, Field Division: 313-393-6000

Houston, TX, Field Division: 281-449-2073

Kansas City, MO, Field Division: 816-421-3440

Los Angeles, CA, Field Division: 213-894-4812

Louisville, KY, Field Division: 502-582-5211

Miami, FL, Field Division: 305-597-4800

Nashville, TN, Field Division: 615-781-5364

New Orleans, LA, Field Division: 504-589-2350

New York, NY, Field Division: 212-466-5145

Philadelphia, PA, Field Division: 215-597-7266

Phoenix, AZ, Field Division: 602-776-5400

San Francisco, CA, Field Division: 415-744-7001

Seattle, WA, Field Division: 206-220-6440

St. Paul, MN, Field Division: 651-290-3092

Tampa, FL, Field Division: 813-228-2021

Washington, DC, Field Division: 202-927-8810

## The Internal Revenue Service (IRS)

The IRS is one of the largest financial institutions in the world and is responsible for enforcing the United States tax laws. In order to investigate such crimes as income tax evasion and international money laundering, the IRS employs over 3,000 law enforcement personnel. Many federal agencies rely on these men and women to infiltrate criminal gangs and activities by following their financial trail. The infamous gangster Al Capone was caught by an IRS special agent for tax evasion...after many other federal agencies were unable to pin a crime on him.

### Special Agent (Criminal Investigator)

These agents are known as "accountants with a badge." They investigate cases involving financial tax crimes, narcotics, organized crime, and public corruption, using the latest computer technology and surveillance techniques. Because some of these cases involve international schemes, agents may find themselves working in IRS outposts in countries such as Germany, Columbia, France, and China. There are seven regional offices and numerous smaller offices located throughout the United States.

#### *Qualifications*

Special agents must be between the ages of 21 and 37 at the time of their appointment, be a U.S. citizen, hold a valid driver's license, have registered with the Selective Service (male applicants only), pass a background investigation, and have a four-year college degree. The IRS also requires "suitability," which means that certain types of convictions, firings from previous employment, and failure to pay federal debt can make a candidate ineligible.

A medical exam is given, which checks vision (must be 20/20 corrected) and hearing, and includes blood tests and urinalysis.

### *Training*

An eight-week course in the basics of criminal investigation is given at the Federal Law Enforcement Training Center in Glynco, Georgia. This is followed by 12 weeks of specialized training in tax law, criminal tax fraud, computer fraud, money laundering, financial fraud schemes, undercover operations, electronic surveillance techniques, forensic sciences, court procedures, and trial witness training. Because the recovery of computer evidence is a crucial part of the job, special agents receive three weeks of training at Glynco, followed by two to three weeks annually in order to keep up with the latest technology.

### *Finding a Job*

Job openings are listed on the Treasury Department and IRS's websites, www.treas.gov, and www.irs.treas.gov. Vacancy announcements contain the address where an application may be sent, but many allow you to use the online application service found on the website. For general information, the websites allow you to speak with an IRS agent and work on your resume in a "resume builder" area. You may also write for information to:

IRS Central Examining Unit (CEU)
P.O. Box 1427
New York, New York 10008
Attention: Chief, Central Examining Unit

## DEPARTMENT OF DEFENSE

Every branch of the United States military maintains its own law enforcement agency. They employ police officers and investigators, whose duties are similar to those of their civilian counterparts. For many of these positions, you must be in the military; however, the Navy and Air Force also hire civilian personnel. For military-hire-only jobs, refer to Chapter 3 for all the necessary information on the enlistment process, on joining the military through attendance at military academies, and on service through the ROTC, National Guard, and Reserves.

Thousands of new military police officers are recruited yearly. Officers uphold the law and prevent crime; they patrol military installations and bases; they take part in undercover surveillance operations; they may work in K9 units; and they staff corrections units (including prison camps maintained during wartime).

Criminal investigators are also hired in large numbers. They work on cases that involve the military crimes of treason, sabotage, and espionage, as well as crimes common to civilians, such as theft and property damage. Intelligence officers and special agents gather information about enemy forces. They may work undercover throughout the world gathering and analyzing intelligence.

## The Army

The Army's investigative arm is known as the Criminal Investigation Division, or CID. CID Agents provide security for key Army and Department of Defense officials. They investigate all felony offenses committed on Army property and alleged felony violations of the Uniform Code of Military Justice committed by soldiers anywhere in the world. Agents also conduct extensive fraud investigations with other Justice Department agencies. They work out of over 200 offices worldwide and must be ready to travel and relocate throughout their careers.

### *Qualifications*

Applicants must be a specialist or sergeant with eight or fewer years of active federal service. Thirty or more semester hours of college are required; a bachelor's degree will put a candidate ahead of those who have not yet gotten a degree. Applicants must also have a score of 110 or higher on the Army's general technical exam. Prior service as a military policeman or police investigator is not required.

### *Training*

To become a CID Agent, the Army requires completion of a 15-week Apprentice Special Agent Course at the U.S. Army Military Police School.

After the course, soldiers spend their first year as an apprentice agent before becoming fully accredited.

### *Finding a Job*

Interested soldiers can receive application packets from any CID office (their headquarters are at Fort Belvoir, Virginia, and they have offices at Forts Bragg, Benning, Hood, and Lewis).

## The Navy

The Navy's Criminal Investigative Service (NCIS) employs 1,600 people, 850 of whom are civilian special agents. They are stationed in 150 locations worldwide. Their duties involve investigating crime, working on counterintelligence, and providing personnel security.

### *Qualifications*

Civilian applicants must:

- be between the ages of 21 and 37
- hold a bachelor's degree
- be in excellent physical condition
- pass a background investigation

### *Training*

Recruits go through nine weeks of Basic Agent Training in Glynco, Georgia. This is followed by six weeks of a special NCIS course; classes include: General Criminal Investigation, Computer Crime Investigation, Foreign Counterintelligence, and Naval Security Programs.

### *Finding a Job*

You can contact the Navy regarding job openings and the application process at 1-800-616-8891, or through their website, www.ncis.navy.mil. The NCIS's field offices are also good points of contact. They are located as follows:

**CAROLINAS FIELD OFFICE**

H-32 Julian C. Smith Boulevard

Camp Lejeune, NC 28547

(910) 451-8071

**GULF COAST FIELD OFFICE**

341 Saufley Street

Pensacola, FL 32508

(904) 452-3835

**HAWAII FIELD OFFICE**

449 South Avenue

Pearl Harbor, HI 96860

(808) 474-1218

**LOS ANGELES FIELD OFFICE**

1317 W. Foothill Boulevard, Suite 120

Upland, CA 91786

(909) 985-2264

**MAYPORT FIELD OFFICE**

P.O. Box 280076

Naval Station

Mayport, FL 32228-0076

(904) 270-5361

**NORFOLK FIELD OFFICE**

1329 Bellinger Boulevard

Norfolk, VA 23511-2395

(804) 444-7327

**NORTHEAST FIELD OFFICE**

344 Meyercord Avenue

Naval Education Training Center

Newport, RI 02841-1607

(401) 841-2241

### NORTHWEST FIELD OFFICE

Land Title Professional Building
9657 Levin Road SW, Suite 220
Silverdale, WA 98383
(360) 396-4460

### SAN DIEGO FIELD OFFICE

Box 368130
3405 Welles Street, Suite 1
San Diego, CA 92136
(619) 556-1364

### WASHINGTON FIELD OFFICE

Washington Naval Yard
Building 200
Washington, DC 20374
(202) 433-3858

## The Air Force

The Air Force Office of Special Investigations (OSI) provides criminal investigation and counterintelligence services to commanders of all air force activities. They employ over 1,600 special agents, 236 of whom are civilians. These agents seek to identify, investigate, and neutralize espionage, terrorism, fraud, and other criminal activities. They have four major priorities:

1. exploit counterintelligence activities for force protection
2. resolve violent crime impacting the Air Force
3. protect Air Force information systems and technologies
4. stop and deter acquisition fraud

### *Training*

The OSI sends its recruits to an 11-week Special Investigator Course at the Special Investigations Academy located at Andrews Air Force Base. This course includes instruction in law, investigative theory, report writing, forensics, and interview techniques. After graduation, agents spend a one-year probationary period in the field. Upon completion of this period, agents may be selected to receive further specialized training in areas such as technical surveillance countermeasures, polygraph, economic crime, or antiterrorism service.

### *Finding a Job*

To begin the application process, contact the OSI at:

Air Force Office of Special Investigations
Public Affairs Office
1535 Command Drive, Suite C-309
Andrews AFB MD 20762-7002
(240) 857-0989

You can also get information on the air force website: www.af.mil.

## DEPARTMENT OF TRANSPORTATION

The major law enforcement employer of the Department of Transportation is the United States Coast Guard. Like the Navy and Air Force, the Coast Guard hires civilians to serve in their Investigative Service Program. Active duty warrant and petty officers, as well as reservists, are also eligible for employment consideration.

### Coast Guard

The Coast Guard is the nation's leading maritime law enforcement agency. Guard personnel are authorized to enforce federal law on waters subject to U.S. jurisdiction, on international waters, and on all vessels subject to U.S. jurisdiction. Their Operational Law Enforcement Mission focuses on four main areas:

1. boating safety
2. drug interdiction

3. living marine resources
4. alien migrant interdiction

Special agents working in the Coast Guard Investigative Service (CGIS) are involved primarily in drug trafficking, due to the amount of narcotics that are smuggled into the country by boat.

They also provide protection for Coast Guard personnel, conduct internal affairs investigations, and grant security clearances to Coast Guard personnel after background investigations are successfully completed.

### *Qualifications*

There is a range of requirements, based on the position and its location. College graduates with prior law enforcement experience have an advantage. As with most other law enforcement jobs, physical fitness, a clean record, and being between the ages of 21 to 37 are all mandatory.

### *Training*

Agent recruits attend courses at the Federal Law Enforcement Training Center in Glynco, Georgia. After the course, they must get a security clearance before beginning duties.

### *Finding a Job*

There is a recruiting page on the Coast Guard website: www.uscg.mil. Job openings are announced under the title "Criminal Investigator" on the OPM website. Or, you can call the Coast Guard at 1-880-438-8724.

## DEPARTMENT OF THE INTERIOR

There are a number of law enforcement positions available with the Department of Interior. Investigators, police officers, rangers, and inspectors are hired by the Fish and Wildlife Service, the Bureau of Land Management, and the Bureau of Indian Affairs. However, the largest employer by far, with the best outlook for future hiring, is the National Park Service.

## National Park Service

Law enforcement careers with the National Park Service include U.S. Park Police Officers and U. S. Park Rangers. Police officers are hired by the National Capitol Region and begin work in the metropolitan Washington, D.C., area. In fact, officers should expect to spend their careers working in large urban areas. Park police prevent, detect, and investigate accidents and crimes; aid people in emergencies; arrest violators; and provide crowd control.

Rangers work in urban, suburban, and rural areas. They are involved with the conservation and use of resources in national parks and other federally managed sites. Rangers enforce laws; investigate violations, complaints, and accidents; protect property; and conduct search and rescue.

### *Qualifications*

Applicants must:

- be between the ages of 21 and 31 (Park Police), or 21 and 37 (Park Ranger)
- have a valid driver's license
- pass a physical exam
- pass a background investigation
- have a bachelor's degree and/or
- two years of work experience

### Training

National Park Service training takes place at the Horace M. Albright Training Center at Grand Canyon National Park, AZ; the Stephen T. Mather Training Center at Harper's Ferry, WV; and at their training Center in Brunswick, GA. Police recruits also take the basic Law Enforcement course at the Federal Law Enforcement Training Center in Glynco, GA. Once formal training is complete, park police and rangers receive on-site training when they begin employment.

### *Finding a Job*

Employment opportunities are listed with the OPM. The OPM administers a test to applicants, and then refers those with the highest scores to the

National Park Service. Check www.opm.gov for information about job openings and test sites/dates.

## INDEPENDENT FEDERAL AGENCIES

This category includes a variety of law enforcement employers, including the U.S. General Services Administration, Environmental Protection Agency, Tennessee Valley Authority, and the U.S. Postal Inspection Service. We will discuss below the largest employers, with the best outlook for future hiring.

### The U.S. General Services Administration

The General Services Administration is one of the three central management agencies in the federal government. Its mission is to provide space, supplies, services, and work environments. There are representatives of the GSA wherever federal employees are at work.

#### Federal Protective Service Officer

The Federal Protective Service (FPS) is the security branch of the U.S. General Services Administration (GSA), a huge government agency that performs numerous managerial functions related to civilian work sites owned or leased by the federal government. One of the GSA's most important functions—that of ensuring the protection of life and property at these work sites nationwide—is carried out by the Federal Protective Service.

The FPS maintains a mobile, uniformed police force of over 800 professionals known as federal protective officers. They enforce laws, provide security services, and perform general policing duties on GSA-controlled federal properties. The FPS also maintains a force of nonuniformed criminal investigators who investigate crimes committed on these properties, often working with local and other law enforcement agencies.

FPS officers' main responsibilities are to establish proper security measures and preserve law and order. They are assigned to civilian work sites that are owned or leased by the federal government, where they protect the employees of and visitors to these work sites as well as the actual physical property, buildings, and grounds.

Patrol duties include checking for signs of intrusion, damage, tampering, or unsafe conditions at the facilities. One assignment is to watch over entrances to these areas to make sure that only federal employees and authorized visitors are admitted. Federal protective officers may also monitor electronic security systems which range from fire alarms to surveillance devices designed to detect intruders, criminal activity, or safety hazards.

Federal protective officers keep the peace and prevent or suppress unlawful conduct. They have the authority to question suspects, issue citations, make arrests, and seize evidence relative to crimes committed on the federal property to which they are assigned. These crimes could include burglary, physical assault, arson, disturbing the peace, instigating a riot, or unlawful assembly. They handle emergencies such as fires, bomb threats, and natural disasters.

#### *Qualifications*

To qualify for this position, you must be a U.S. citizen of at least 21 years of age. You'll need to pass a written test, a personal interview, a physical examination (including vision and hearing tests), a drug screening, and a background investigation. Other requirements include at least one year of police experience, or an equivalent amount of college education as determined by the Federal Protective Service.

#### *Training*

Trainees participate in an eight-week police training course at the Federal Law Enforcement Training Center in Glynco, Georgia. Specialized training is also provided in crowd and riot control techniques and in performing police functions that have an impact on national security.

#### *Finding a Job*

The written test is administered by the OPM. If you pass this test, you will be put on an eligibility list for Federal Protective Officer positions. More information on testing and application procedures is available through the nearest FPS office, listed below. You can also contact:

Office of Federal Protective Service
1800 F Street NW, Room 2341
Washington, DC 20405-0002
(202) 501-0907

## FEDERAL PROTECTIVE SERVICE DIVISION OFFICES

**GSA, Federal Protective Service Division**
Thomas P. O'Neil Federal Building
10 Causeway Street, Room 935
Boston, MA 02222-1098
(607) 565-5784

**GSA, Federal Protective Service Division**
26 Federal Plaza, Room 17-130
New York, NY 10278-0013
(212) 264-4255

**GSA, Federal Protective Service Division**
Wanamaker Plaza
100 Penn Square, Room 732
Philadelphia, PA 19107-3396
(215) 656-6060

**GSA, Federal Protective Service Division**
Peachtree Summit Building
401 West Peachtree Street NW, Suite 2339
Atlanta, GA 30365-2250
(404) 331-5132

**GSA, Federal Protective Service Division**
Kluczynski Federal Building
230 South Dearborn Street, Room 3540
DPN: 35-5 Mail Room
Chicago, IL 60604-1503
(312) 353-1496

**GSA, Federal Protective Service Division**

1500 East Bannister Road, Room 2151

Kansas City, MO 64131-3088

(816) 926-7025

**GSA, Federal Protective Service Division**

819 Taylor Street, Room 12A01

Ft. Worth, TX 76102-6105

(817) 978-3359

**GSA, Federal Protective Service Division**

Denver Federal Center, Building 41

West 6th Avenue & Kipling Street

Denver, CO 80225-0546

(303) 236-7965

**GSA, Federal Protective Service Division**

450 Golden Gate Avenue, 5th floor- Room 5474

San Francisco, CA 94102-3400

(415) 522-3440

**GSA, Federal Protective Service Division**

400 15th Street SW

Auburn, WA 98000-6599

(253) 931-7521

**GSA, Federal Protective Service Division**

Building 74, Room 110

Southeast Federal Center

Third and M Streets, SE

Washington, DC 2040-0001

(202) 690-9632

## U.S. Postal Inspection Service

This is the law enforcement unit of the U.S. Postal Service, with jurisdiction over crimes involving the postal system and its employees. Postal inspectors deal with the theft, delay of delivery, and destruction of mail. They also investigate those who violate laws by mailing obscene material, such as child pornography, and hazardous material, such as bombs and illegal drugs. The Postal Service currently employs over 2,200 inspectors.

### *Qualifications*

Applicants must be between the ages of 21 and 36 and have held a valid driver's license for two or more years. They must be able to write and speak English clearly and cannot have any felony convictions or misdemeanor domestic violence convictions. The Postal Service requires drug screening, a background investigation, and polygraph test of all potential employees. Vision must be correctable to 20/30 in one eye and 20/40 in the other, and, as with many law enforcement positions, radial keratotomy surgery is disqualifying.

Those interested in becoming a postal inspector must be willing to relocate. A bachelor's degree and work experience is also necessary. The degree can be in any field, but prior employment must include:

- postal service experience, or
- internal audit experience, or
- law enforcement experience, or
- military (officer) experience

A law degree or foreign language expertise can satisfy the work experience requirement.

### *Training*

Postal Inspector trainees attend a 14-week Postal Inspector Course in Potomac, MD. Instruction includes: investigative techniques, defensive tactics, firearms training, legal matters, search and seizure, arrest techniques, court procedures, and postal operations.

### *Finding a Job*

To request application materials, write to:

U. S. Postal Inspection Service
475 L'Enfant Plaza SW, Room 3100
Washington, DC 20260-2100
(202) 268-4267 or
1-800-JOBUSPS

## Administrative Office of the Court

The law enforcement position available with this office is United States Probation Officer. The Administrative Office of the Court oversees District Courts throughout the county.

### U.S. Probation Officer

These officers work with individuals convicted of federal offenses. Probation officers investigate defendants' prior records, their backgrounds, and their offense(s), and prepare reports for the court. They assess offenders for probability of future criminal behavior and their ability to pay restitution, fines, and costs of prosecution, incarceration, and supervision.

Probation officers testify in court and serve as a resource to the court of information regarding offenders. They supervise offenders to make sure that they adhere to their sentences, get the correctional treatment they need, and are a reduced risk to the community. Officers are in contact with dangerous criminals on a daily basis.

### *Qualifications*

Applicants must:

- be between the ages of 21 and 37
- maintain excellent physical condition, with good distance vision and hearing
- successfully pass an FBI background check
- undergo drug screening

- have a bachelor's degree in a field such as criminal justice, criminology, psychology, sociology, human relations, or business or public administration
- have three years of specialized work experience in fields such as probation, parole, corrections, criminal investigations, or work in substance/addiction treatment, or
- combine a graduate degree with one year of specialized experience

### *Training*

Recruits attend courses at the Federal Law Enforcement Training Center in Glynco, Georgia.

### *Finding a Job*

Openings are listed on the website www.uscourts.gov/employment. You may also write for information to:

Mr. Richard A. Houck, Jr., Chief
United States Probation Officer
333 Constitution Avenue NW, Room 2800
Washington, DC 20001-2866

## INSIDE TRACK

**Who:** Damon Katz
**What:** Special Agent
**Where:** FBI
**How long:** 4 years
**Degree:** Bachelor's degree in government from small private college; law degree from large northeastern university

Like many boys, I played a lot of cops and robbers. But I didn't think seriously about law enforcement as a career until I was 18, when some local officers in town suggested that I apply for a position as a summer officer. I got the job and liked it. I stayed interested in law enforcement through college and law school, then applied for a job with the FBI.

Getting into the FBI can take a long time. The requirements are strict, and the process has many steps. In my case, it took more than 18 months to get appointed to a class. The hardest part was waiting for word. Because our budget is set by congress, the money available for new hires varies from year to year, and there can be temporary hiring freezes. My advice is to put in your application and get on with your life. At some point, hiring always resumes.

The work of an FBI agent is generally slower-paced than uniformed police work. As a rule, our investigations are more intricate and lengthy, and they require a daily commitment. We proceed slowly and methodically, and it often takes months or years to make a case. For someone who likes a different task every day, with quick turnover and fast cases, I would recommend uniformed work, especially in a city or large town, rather than with the FBI.

For college students interested in an FBI career, I suggest majoring in a subject that really interests you. There is no one college program that best qualifies you for the FBI. We have agents who majored in English, computers, art history, biology, and many other subjects. I cannot stress enough the importance of learning and doing what interests you. If you like your subject matter, you will do better at it. After college, you will need work experience and/or a graduate degree. Contact your nearest FBI Field Office at that point for up-to-date hiring requirements. The FBI accepts candidates between the ages of 23 and 37, so there is a lot of time for someone to get hired.

# CHAPTER Six

## APPLYING FOR THE JOB

THIS CHAPTER gives you detailed advice from recruiting experts on how to put together everything you've learned in order to successfully market your skills and experience to future employers. You'll learn the secrets behind the law enforcement hiring process, how to earn the respect and admiration of background investigators, and how to survive intimidating oral interviews.

**YOU HAVE** learned about how to prepare to be a candidate for a job in law enforcement, the types of jobs available and where to find them, and what the risk and rewards of those jobs are. The next step is to apply for one of those jobs. This chapter is devoted to helping you come up with a blueprint for success.

### EXPERT ADVICE

We polled law enforcement recruiters and managers across the nation about their experiences with both top-notch applicants and ones who didn't measure up, and then boiled their experiences down to a few basic suggestions.

## Education

The importance of education can't be emphasized enough. Most recruiters we talked to were partial to hiring applicants with college degrees, both because law enforcement hiring trends indicate the need, and because they thought college graduates made better officers and agents.

Gary Margolis, chief of police at the University of Vermont, and former training coordinator at the Vermont Police Academy, says

> When I'm hiring, I look for someone who's well-educated. I can't stress this enough—if you want to be in law enforcement, go to college and get a degree.

Our experts also mentioned that they look not only at whether or not you have a degree, but how you got it. You need to attend class regularly and get good grades. Participate as fully as possible in life on campus or in your community. This means you should volunteer and join teams or organizations that can give you some of the skills you will need later. If you need to work while going to school, do your best at both. Investigators will also want to know how you felt and what you learned from the college experience.

## Employment

A stable job history is also very important, according to those we polled. Background investigators will be calling your past employers to find out how you handled your responsibilities. (If you are just starting out in the workforce, keep this in mind as you choose your place of employment.) They'll ask if you got to work on time, how you performed your duties, and how well you got along with customers, coworkers, and supervisors. Your work history is one of the scales they will use to measure your level of maturity.

If you've been in the workforce long enough to have a list of previous employers, be ready to explain how you handled yourself, why you made the decisions you did, and what you've learned from the experience. You may be asked what you'd do differently if you had it all to do over. As for the job you hold now, do everything you can to make it a positive experience. You want a good recommendation from your employer, so it is important that you get to work on time, take pride in your work, and maintain good relations with coworkers and clients or customers.

## Finances

The professionals we talked to all agreed that how you handle your financial affairs says a lot about how you handle responsibility. Some told us that they flatly refuse to consider applicants who have excessive amounts of debt or who have a history of financial irresponsibility (i.e., hot checks, failure to pay bills in a timely manner, and so on). Others said that although they may not disqualify applicants for shaky finances, they can guarantee that these applicants will spend a lot of their oral interview explaining their past financial decisions.

If you have financial problems, your future employer will want to know what you are doing to correct them, and if you are taking responsibility for your actions. Use the services of a credit counselor (which are often free), get rid of high-interest credit cards, and put yourself on a budget before you apply for a job. Although your past mistakes will still be on your record, you can show that you are now on the right track.

One veteran recruiter in Chicago gave the best advice for those with a poor financial record:

> Don't wait for me to point out your problems and tell you what to do to get your life in shape. If your problems are that obvious to us and to everyone else who knows you, then you need to get your life in order before you start our process. Fix what you can and be ready to talk about the rest.

## Community Involvement

Although volunteer activities are important for every candidate, they can be especially helpful for students who have yet to hold a paying job. Volunteer for activities that will put you in contact with people of all types and ages. If you like kids and sports, help coach a Little League baseball team or a Peewee football team. There are programs through which you can help the elderly, young children, and many groups in between. For example, look into organizations such as Big Brother/Big Sister and Scouting. Contact your local IRS office regarding volunteer programs that exist to help older men and women with their tax forms. Police Explorers, a program chartered by local police departments, offers a way to get hands-on experience in your future occupation, serve your community, and receive leadership training. Search the Internet using the term "police explorers" to find out if there is a program at a police department near you.

Getting involved in your community through volunteering will provide you with an answer when the oral board asks you to describe a time when you helped others. The more involved you get, the more life experience you'll build, and the more points you will score with your future employer.

**IN THE NEWS**

In a survey conducted by the U.S. Department of Justice, 58% of the general public was found to have a "great deal" of confidence in the police. Compare that figure to 57% for organized religion, and 45% for the Presidency.

## Character

As you've read in previous chapters, law enforcement professionals are held to a higher personal standard. Your thoughts, opinions, past deeds, and experiences with friends, family, and coworkers all will be closely scrutinized by background investigators and by those who have the final authority to hire you. Your personal ethics and integrity will be important criteria in the recruiters' consideration of your candidacy. There's no room for those who can't take responsibility for their actions or tell the truth. And lying about anything during the hiring process will almost certainly get you disqualified, no matter what kind of excuse you present. (You'll hear more on this issue later in the chapter.) All the professionals we polled agreed that no one expects you to be perfect and not to have made mistakes, but you are expected to own up to them and to have learned from them. As old-fashioned as it may sound, employers want to hire men and women who will bring honor to the profession. Sheriff Don Farley of the Rockingham County Sheriff's Department sums it up:

> I expect law enforcement officers to perform their duties in a professional manner that will earn the respect of those they serve. A person who wears the uniform is a representative of the people who demand a safe and secure place to work and raise a family. It is every officer's charge to perform his or her job and to live their personal life in a manner that is an example of what is right.

## PLAN AHEAD

Now that it is clear what is expected of you, you can formulate a plan for success. Whether you are about to enter the field, or are still in school with a few years before you begin a job search, there are things you can do right now to get ready for your career in law enforcement. Below are guidelines for two groups: those in high school or college, and those who are no longer in school.

### Plan A: For Those in High School or College

- do well in school and get your diploma
- begin a lifelong habit of staying in good physical condition
- stay out of trouble: drinking, drug use, vandalism, stealing, and other illegal behavior could make it hard or impossible to have the career of your choice
- if applicable, be careful with your checkbook and credit cards; pay your bills on time

- when you get a job, do your best: show up on time; treat your boss, coworkers, and the public with respect; build a reputation you'll be proud to talk about with your future employer
- get involved in your community by volunteering
- if you are in high school, begin to think about and plan for college and/or military service
- if you are in college, consider an internship such as those suggested in Chapter 2

### Plan B: For Those Out of School

- follow all applicable advice in Plan A (if you didn't graduate from high school, get a GED immediately)
- if your finances are in trouble, seek advice from an expert — there is plenty of help available at no cost; get a copy of your credit report and work to straighten it out
- if you have legal problems, fix what you can, and be prepared to explain the rest; consult an attorney to help figure out your options
- evaluate yourself as a candidate: identify strengths and weaknesses by using tools such as those found at www.usacareers.opm.gov; work on weaknesses
- prepare a resume showing your education and job experience(s); don't spend a lot of money on expensive formatting and paper—you may not need to submit it to anyone, but it will help you when it comes time to fill out applications

## THE APPLICATION PROCESS

This section deals with the nine sections of the application process. Note that depending on the job you are applying for, the order of these sections may be different, and one or more may not be required at all. Chapter 4 dealt with finding out where jobs are and how to get an application. When you use this information to make contact your future employer, ask for an overview of the entire process as it applies to the job you are interested in.

## The Application

The first step in the process of becoming a law enforcement officer is filling out an application. Depending on the employer, this form can be anywhere from 1 to 20 pages long. The initial paperwork will be screened to determine whether you meet the minimum hiring qualifications. You may be asked to fill out an application to take the written test, with a more detailed application to come later if you pass.

As mentioned earlier, you should check on whether the department to which you're applying accepts resumes before you spend your time and money putting one together. Many police, state police, sheriff's departments, and corrections agencies do not accept resumes. On the other hand, many federal agencies do, and they ask for them to follow specific formats. (The Office of Personnel Management has a resume format on hand that you can have sent to you, or you can use the online resume format on their webpage.) Check the job announcement closely to see what is required.

Federal agencies that go through the OPM to hire their employees are just as serious about their applications as other law enforcement agencies. They expect your paperwork to be carefully filled out correctly, with every direction heeded. For example, the general information section of the OPM's Optional Application for Federal Employment states:

> You may apply for most federal jobs with a resume, this Optional Application for Federal Employment, or other written format. If your resume or application does not provide all the information requested on this form and in the job vacancy announcement, you may lose consideration for a job. Type or print clearly in dark ink. Help speed the selection process by keeping your application brief and sending only the requested information.

The OPM handles thousands of applications for federal employment, and you can bet they don't have much patience for sloppy, incomplete paper work. There are too many qualified people competing for your job for you to take a chance with this part of the process.

**JUST THE FACTS**

It can cost a police department $60,000 or more to recruit, hire, train and equip an officer. This amount is double the officer's first year salary, which is why departments use such a thorough application process. They need to eliminate those who won't be able to handle the job well before they attend the academy.

## The Written Exam

Most agencies give written exams as the next step in the application process, though in some cases a background interview may come first. (By putting the background interview first, agencies save themselves the expense of testing applicants who don't meet the basic qualifications.) As a rule, if you don't pass the test, you are out of the process. If you do, your score may be used to rank you on the eligibility list. In some cases, your score alone will determine your rank, while in others it's combined with physical agility, oral interview scores, and/or other testing results (points may be added here for military service). The exam announcement will usually let you know how the ranking works.

The written exams test basic skills and aptitudes: your reading comprehension, your writing ability, your ability to follow directions, your judgment and reasoning, memory, and/or math skills. On the federal level, you may be asked to take a test such as the Treasury Enforcement Agent (TEA) exam. This exam tests your judgment, logic, planning, and communication skills. Not all federal positions require it, but many agencies, such as the ATF, do.

Before giving you the exam, some agencies require that you study written material (study guides) in advance and then answer questions during the exam based on the study guide. Some of these study guides have to do with the law and police or corrections procedures, or they may contain photos and drawings for you to memorize.

Exams can be anxiety-producing, but they're given for good reasons.

Departments need officers and agents who can read, understand, and make decisions based on complex written materials such as laws, policy handbooks, and regulations. You can't do the job without being able to write incident reports, affidavits, and other documents that are clear and correct for court or other formal legal proceedings. And you will need sound mathematical skills for such basic tasks as adding up the value of stolen goods or calculating the street price of a kilo of cocaine confiscated in a drug raid. Because of the importance placed on your scores, you need to take the exams seriously, but be relaxed enough to think clearly and correctly. Becoming familiar with the test format and contents will improve your performance.

Most exams are given in multiple-choice format, like the ones given in high school or college. You will be given an exam book and an answer sheet on which you'll have to fill in circles or squares with a number-two pencil. A few agencies, particularly municipal police departments, will also have you write an essay or a mock police report. There are a number of books and software programs which contain test-taking tips and allow you to take practice exams. Some of this information can also be found on the Internet. Become a more confident test-taker by using any or all of these materials. Applicants are generally notified in writing about the results of the exam. Some agencies grade tests with scanners and can tell you immediately what your score is, although it is rare to find out your ranking until everyone's test has been graded; it is more common to get results through the mail.

## The Physical Agility Test

Most agencies put applicants through an agility test. Some are complicated, some are not. For example, applicants with the Phoenix Police Department (AZ) are asked to scale a six-foot block wall, do a 1.5 mile run, sit-ups, and bench press. Applicants are expected to perform the events according to their age, sex, and body weight ratio (for the bench press). On the other end of the spectrum, the Austin Police Department (TX) has a physical test consisting of a timed obstacle course 440 yards in length. The course is designed to simulate a foot pursuit and consists of 17 separate components, ending with the applicant dragging a 165-pound dummy 15 feet. No matter whose test you take, you can expect a fair amount of running, some lifting or other upper-body strength requirements, and often a test of hand strength that helps to determine whether you'll be able to handle a gun.

The agility test is designed to find out whether you're in good enough shape to do well in the physical training part of the academy, and later, in your career. The agility test can weed out those who would not be able to meet the standard set at the academy. As discussed in previous chapters, when you know you want a career in law enforcement, you should begin an exercise program that keeps you in shape aerobically and improves your strength and flexibility. The department you're applying to may offer physical abilities classes that can train you specifically in those skills the department is looking for. It pays to take advantage of these classes if you think you need help preparing for this test.

## The Personal History Statement and Background Investigation

Most agencies ask that you fill out the Personal History Statement before you get to any of the other stages in the hiring process, because it is arguably the most important. The statement, and the following background investigation, will allow the agency to which you are applying a way to evaluate whether you are the type of person they are looking to hire.

Use the following guidelines to prepare your statement, beginning with an outline of the steps involved:

1. Make lists of information regarding places of residence, employment, and driving history.
2. Gather necessary documents.
3. Organize yourself and make copies of the form before and after you fill it out.
4. Read all questions through first, and ask questions if something is unclear.
5. Answer thoroughly and honestly.
6. Choose good personal references.
7. Make a final copy that has been checked and rechecked for errors, is neat, and has followed all directions.

### Being Prepared—Now

Start by making a list of every address you've lived at, then move on to your employment history. Create a list of every part-time and full-time job you've had since your working life began. Next, research your driving history. You'll be asked by some departments to list every traffic ticket you ever received in any state or country, whether on a military post or on civilian roadways. Some may ask you to list only moving violations (these include speeding, running red lights, and unsafe lane changes), while other departments want to see both moving violations and tickets for expired license plates, failure to wear seat belts, and expired automobile insurance. The information you gathered will be used in one form or another every time you apply for a different law enforcement position, so make copies. You may have to change the lists slightly to conform to what the agency asks you for, but your homework will already be done. You will have eliminated a time-consuming portion of the process of completing the Personal History Statement.

You should also gather the following documents:

1. birth certificate
2. Social Security card
3. DD 214 (if you are a veteran)
4. naturalization papers (if applicable)
5. high school diploma or GED certificate
6. high school transcripts
7. college transcripts
8. current driver's license(s)
9. current copies of driving records
10. current consumer credit reports

If you don't have certified copies of these documents, start calling or writing the proper authorities now to find out how to get them. If you lost your Social Security card, go to the Social Security office in your community and arrange for a new one. Legal documents often take anywhere from six to eight weeks for delivery, and you may not have that much time if you have already received and started on your Personal History Statement. If you are already near your deadline and know you won't be able to submit the

Personal History Statement with all the required documents, ask the agency what you should do. Many departments will tell you to attach a memo to your application outlining your problem and what you have done about it.

You should also call the recruiting department and ask how they require these documents to be delivered so you'll know what to do. For example, official college transcripts will probably go directly from the college to the agency you're applying to.

Other questions you should ask are:

1. Do they need photocopies or original documents?
2. Will they return my original if I send it?
3. How recent does the credit history have to be?
4. What is the most recent copy they will accept of my college transcript?

### Organize and Make Copies

Before you set pen to paper, make several copies of the personal history form. After you have made them, put away the original. You'll be using the photocopy as a working draft and a place to make mistakes. Eventually, you will transfer all the information from the practice copy onto the original. Once the original is complete, you should make even more copies. Being well-prepared can save you the hassle of having to complete the statement all over again if, for instance, your recruiter misplaces your one-and-only copy.

### Read and Answer Questions Thoroughly

Reading questions and instructions carefully is crucial to successfully completing the Personal History Statement. Certain words should leap off the page, such as "all," "every," "any," and "each." When in doubt, list anything you think could possibly fall into the category on which you are working. The best advice is to ask if you don't know.

### Personal References

These are the people who will be able to give the background investigator the best picture of you as a whole person. Some Personal History Statements ask you to list at least five people as references; some only ask for three. You also may be given a specific time limit for how long you have to have known these people before listing them.

The Personal References Section is one area where you really want to make the investigator's job easy. You want the investigator to talk to people who know you well, who can comment on your hobbies, interests, personality, and ability to interact with others. Try to choose friends who will be honest, open, and sincere.

### The Final Copy

Because most departments score you on the appearance of the Personal History Statement, is it important to make your final copy error-free and as neat as possible. You may find it useful to have these items on hand:

1. a dictionary
2. a grammar handbook
3. a good pen (or pencil—whichever the directions tell you to use)
4. the eye of an editor (check and recheck your drafts before making the final copy)

Remember, this is not a document to take lightly, especially now that you are aware of the power your statement holds over your potential career. It is important that you:

- carefully follow instructions
- be honest and open about your past and present
- provide accurate information
- choose excellent personal references
- turn in presentable, error-free documentation
- submit all documents on time

## Polygraph Testing

Some agencies use polygraph testing as part of their hiring process. Those that don't require it as a routine part of their investigation will reserve the right to use it if questions arise during your background check. Though some people call the polygraph machine a "lie detector," there really is no such thing. What the polygraph detects is changes in heart and respiratory rates, blood pressure, and galvanic skin resistance (how much you're perspiring). A cuff like the one your doctor uses to take your blood pressure will be wrapped around your arm. Rubber tubes wrapped around your trunk will measure your breathing, and clips on your fingers or palm will measure skin response. The test operates on the theory that people who are consciously lying get nervous and are betrayed by their involuntary bodily responses.

You can't fail the test because of nervousness. It is normal to be a little anxious about this, and the polygraph takes this into account. After the polygraph examiner explains the whole process to you, she will ask you a series of questions to establish a baseline both for when you're telling the truth and for when you're not. For instance, the examiner might tell you to answer "no" to every question asked and then ask you whether your name is George (if it isn't) and whether you drove to the examination today (if you did).

All questions in a polygraph exam are in yes-or-no form. You will be told in advance what every question will be. Some questions will be easy, such as "Are you wearing sneakers?" The questions that really count will be the ones that relate to your fitness to be a law enforcement officer. You probably will have been over any problematic areas with the background investigator or other interviewers before, so just tell the truth and try to relax.

## The Oral Interview and Selection Boards

There are a few similarities between civilian and law enforcement job interviews. Both employers are looking for the most qualified people for the job: reliable, honest, hardworking, dependable men and women. Both expect applicants to show up on time for their interviews dressed and acting professionally. When you enter a law enforcement oral interview board, however, you will realize that the interviewers have more than a superficial interest in you and your past experiences. The board will also have your Personal History Statement and an investigator's report about you in their hands when the interview begins.

You will be facing a panel of at least two people. Some agencies also have civilian personnel specialists on their boards, but most interview boards will be made up of experienced law enforcement officers. These board members will be using the information provided on your Personal History Statement and the investigator's report to formulate questions about your background and personal accomplishments.

Border Patrol Agent Jeremy Farner remembers a little of his oral board interview:

> I had two people on my board, I think. It was very difficult, very stressful. They were very "pushy" for their answers and second-guessed everything I said.

The way the interview is conducted can vary, depending on the department to which you applied. You may be asked a few questions similar to those you've experienced on civilian employment interviews: Why do you want this job? Why do you want to work for this agency? You will also be asked questions resulting from the background investigation.

The trend is for more local and state-level agencies to put standardized questions on their oral boards. They ask each candidate the same questions, and when the interview is over the board rates each candidate on a set scale. These standardized questions help the interviewers reach a more objective conclusion about the candidates they have seen. Scores are usually added to the other test scores that make up your eligibility ranking.

The members of the oral board can ask you just about any question that comes to mind. Applying for a job in public safety puts you in a different league than the civilian-sector applicant. Federal and state laws prohibit civilian employers from seeking certain information about their applicants, but law enforcement agencies can ask you any question that has a bearing on your mental stability, your integrity, your honesty, your character, your reputation in the community, and your ability to do the physical tasks common to the job.

If you follow the guidelines and advice in this chapter, you can avoid making many of the mistakes that can eliminate other well-qualified candidates. You will also be ahead of the applicant who has the same qualifications you have, but who doesn't know to how to prepare for an oral interview board.

### What Is the Board Looking For?

The most important qualities in the eyes of the interview board are:

- integrity
- honesty
- reliability
- maturity
- common sense
- good judgement
- compassion
- competence

Here are a few words of explanation about some of these qualities:

- Integrity, Honesty, and Reliability

The board will be looking to discover if you have the right kind of character to serve your community and to work well with department. Police departments are under scrutiny in the wake of corruption scandals, and they are on the watch for any candidates who might show signs of dishonesty, or a lack of integrity. One of the most important things you can do throughout the hiring process is to be honest. Even if something in your record does not show you in the best light, you will do far more damage to your chances if it is discovered that you lied, or even slightly misrepresented something in your record. And remember that many departments conduct very thorough background checks, so it is quite likely that any misrepresentation of the truth will be uncovered.

Your integrity is also extremely important. The board will be looking to see that you adhere to a strict code of moral conduct. Having integrity means that you are incorruptible, which is essential for any person who wants to uphold the law in their community.

Finally, a candidate must demonstrate that they are reliable. This quality will be evident throughout your record: your work history, your academic record, your personal life, and your finances can all be examined to see if you are reliable. The board will be looking to see that you meet your obligations. For example, showing up on time to your current job without fail will demonstrate that you are reliable. Likewise meeting your family and financial obligations is evidence of your dependability. A police department functions as a team and police officers often work as partners. It is crucial to the safety of the other officers and to the effectiveness of the department that each officer is completely reliable.

► Maturity, Common Sense, and Good Judgment

The question here is will an oral board think you have enough life experience for them to be willing to take a chance on hiring you. Law enforcement agencies have never been as liability-conscious as they are today. Incidents like the Rodney King trial and subsequent Los Angeles riots have heightened the liability awareness of law enforcement agencies around the country.

This concern haunts personnel, recruiters, background investigators, oral interview boards, and everyone who has anything to do with deciding who gets a badge. The first question you hear when trouble arises is: "How did that person get hired here anyway?" Consequently, agencies are scrutinizing applicants more closely than ever before and they are leaning toward individuals who have proven track records in employment, academics, volunteer work, and community involvement.

Signing up for volunteer work shows your willingness to take on responsibility and eagerness to help the community. If you are still living at home with your parents, be able to demonstrate the ways in which you are responsible to them. If you are on your own, but living with roommates, talk to the board about this experience and how it has helped you to learn to handle conflict. You may want to work on your communication skills before going to the board. If you are young, you will have a greater need to be open and allow the board to see you as a worthy investment.

► Compassion

Oral interview boards are faced with the formidable task of hiring individuals who have the skills and talents equal to the demands of modern law enforcement. The most highly sought-after individuals are those who are good with people. As Gary Margolis, chief of police at the University of Vermont says:

> I can't afford to have someone on the force who isn't people-oriented. Your success as a police officer is based on how well you get along with others. If you aren't aware of people's emotions, there will be complaints coming in about it.

The board will be looking for evidence that you can deal well with people who may be in a crisis. You need to be able to make a connection with them, and understand and respect their emotions.

- Competence

Your prior job experience and education can give clues as to how well you will be able to perform the duties of a law enforcement job. During the interview, you will also be able to show your interviewers that you have what it takes to work without constant supervision. You should come across as confident (taking into consideration the nervousness that is a normal part of being interviewed!) and capable. Law enforcement, like many other fields, has to utilize and keep up with technology. Computers are here to stay. You should already be familiar with them, but most importantly, you should show that you have the desire and the ability to learn new things in order to keep up with the changes new technology brings.

### How to Prepare

Preparation for the oral interview board should begin with the decision to apply for a job. From the moment you first make contact with a law enforcement agency, everything you say and do will potentially raise questions for the oral interview board. Even when you walk through the doors of the recruiting office to pick up an application, you have the opportunity to make a lasting impression, because the professionals who deal with you are trained to notice and remember people and details.

- dress neatly and professionally each time you make visual contact with the department where you want to work

- make every telephone call to the agency another opportunity to make a good impression; rehearse and/or write down what you want to say before you call
- ask questions from a list you make up ahead of time, and listen carefully to the response without interruption

Once you are notified that you will be interviewed, more intense and specific preparations should be made. Begin by carefully reviewing your Personal History Statement. Few of the questions during your oral board interview should come as a surprise if you have taken the time to do this. Think carefully think about each piece of information, and how questions could be generated from it.

For example, if one of the questions on the application directed you to list any instances when you've been fired from a job, think about how you would respond if you were asked: "Mr. Smith, can you tell the board why you were fired from Tread Lightly Tire Shop in 1993?" Although you may have previously told the investigator why you were fired, the board will want to hear it for themselves.

Pay particular attention to the weaknesses you had to include on the statement. It is likely that you will be asked about them either specifically, or in a more general way. Do not pay any attention to consultants or books suggesting that you downplay, or deny having, weaknesses. If an oral board member asks you to list weaknesses and you cannot think of any, he or she will be more than happy to use your Personal History Statement to illustrate any weaknesses you aren't able to identify. You should be able to list them in the same unhesitating manner in which you list your strengths. You should also be able to tell the board what you are doing to correct or compensate for those weaknesses.

If you have a fear of public speaking, you should practice as much as possible with friends or family members putting you through mock interviews. Strongly consider taking a speech class at a nearby community college or through an adult education course. At the very least, have a friend ask you questions about yourself and have them give you a completely candid critique of your performance. Then practice your speaking skills and learn to correct any bad habits your friend pointed out to you.

Practice is one of the keys to success for an oral board interview. One effective technique is to mentally place yourself in a situation and visualize how you want to act or respond when the pressure is on. Some professionals call this mental exercise "What if...," and they use this technique to formulate a plan of action for those times when split-second decisions are needed. Visualizing a successful performance can help trigger that response once you're in the actual situation. This technique will work for you if you take the time to practice it.

### The Day of the Interview

Arrive before the scheduled interview. An early arrival shows you planned ahead for emergencies (flat tires, wrong turns, etc.), that you got there in enough time to prepare yourself mentally for what you are about to do, and that you place as much value on other people's time as on your own.

Dress for success. The initial impression you make on board members is in your hands, and this is the perfect opportunity to score points without even opening your mouth. Men should wear a business suit (or at least dress pants and a jacket), a white shirt, tie, and polished shoes. Women should also wear a business suit and polished shoes. Do not wear high heels or carry a large purse. Makeup and jewelry should be tasteful and kept to a minimum.

To go along with your professional appearance, act in a professional manner. Focus on eliminating "yeah" and "nah" from your vocabulary, and replacing them with "yes" and "no." Polite behavior in general will help to create a positive impression.

No doubt you realize that an oral interview board sees many, many applicants when a department is in the hiring phase. Most boards typically schedule five or six interviews each day. Some departments schedule interviews one day a week, while other departments have interviews every day of the week. You may be talking to people who are quite tired of listening. That means the "little things" take on an extra importance. Dr. Rick Bradstreet estimates that he has sat on thousands of interview boards during his career as a police psychologist. When asked what the top three things an applicant can do wrong in an oral interview are, he replies:

> Number one is to get indignant about the questions that are being asked; number two is to give an answer to a question and then defend it to the death because they fear they'll look wishy-washy if they change it; and number three is to give vague responses to questions to try not to commit to an answer.

## Questions—Real-life Examples

What kind of questions are they going to ask? That is what everyone is really worried about with regard to the interview. What follows are samples of the five basic types of questions asked by interviewers:

- open-ended questions
- obvious questions
- fishing expeditions
- situational/ethics queries
- role playing

### *Open-Ended Questions*

These are the ones you are most likely to be asked. An example of an open-ended question is:

BOARD MEMBER: "Mr. Jones, can you tell the board about your Friday-night bowling league?"

Board members like these questions because it gives them an opportunity to see how articulate you are and how you think. This is also a way for them to ease into more specific questions. For example:

BOARD MEMBER: "Mr. Jones, can you tell the board about your Friday-night bowling league?"
JONES: "Yes ma'am. I've been bowling in this league for about two years. We meet every Friday night around 6 P.M. and bowl until about 8:30 P.M.

I like it because it gives me something to do with friends I may not otherwise get to see because everyone is so busy. It also gives me time to spend with my wife. We're in first place right now and I like it that way."

BOARD MEMBER: "Oh, congratulations. You must be a pretty competitive bowler."

JONES: "Yes ma'am, I am. I like to win and I take the game pretty seriously."

BOARD MEMBER: "How do you react when your team loses, Mr. Jones?"

That one series of questions generates enough information for the board to draw many conclusions about Mr. Jones. They can see that he likes to interact with his friends, that he thinks spending time with his wife is a high priority, and that competition and winning are important to him. Mr. Jones' answers open up an avenue for the board to explore how he reacts to disappointment, and if he is able to articulate his feelings and reactions. They'll get a good idea of his temperament.

Open-ended questions allow the board to fish around for information, but this is not a negative. You should seize these opportunities to open up to the board and give them an idea of who you are.

### *Obvious Questions*

Everyone in the room already knows the answer to this type of question. For example:

BOARD MEMBER: "Mr. Jones, you were in the military for four years?"

JONES: "Yes sir, I was in the Marines from 1982 until 1986."

BOARD MEMBER: "Why did you leave?"

The obvious question is used as a way to give the applicant a chance to warm up and to be alerted to which area the board is about to explore. It is also a way for the board to verify the information they've been provided. Board members and background investigators can misread or misunderstand the information they receive. Being aware of this, board members will be careful to confirm details with you during the interview.

### *Fishing Expeditions*

The fishing expedition question is nerve-wracking to answer. You aren't certain why they are asking it or where it came from, and they aren't giving out any clues. For example:

BOARD MEMBER: "Mr. Jones, in your application you stated that you've never been detained by police. (Usually they will pause for effect and then get to the point.) You've never been detained?"

In the example above, if the applicant has been detained by police and has failed to list this on his application, then he'll be wondering if the board knows this happened. The odds are very high that the board does indeed know the answer before it asks the question. If the applicant has never been detained then paranoia is certain to set in. Did someone on his list of references lie to the background investigator? Did someone on the board misread his application? These questions race through his mind as the board scrutinizes him.

Chances are, the board is simply fishing to see what he'll say. In any event, don't let these questions cause you a dilemma; if you are honest there can be no dilemma. You simply MUST tell the truth at all times in an oral board. At stake is your integrity, reputation, and, not least of all, your career. Don't try to guess why the board is asking a question. Your only job is to answer truthfully and openly.

### *Situational/Ethics Queries*

These questions begin with the words "What would you do if,...." For example:

BOARD MEMBER: "Mr. Jones, assume you are a police officer and you are on your way to back up another officer at the scene of a burglary at a clothing store. You walk in just in time to see him pick up a small bottle of men's cologne and put it into his pocket. What do you do?"

Some oral boards are almost exclusively one situational question after another. Other departments may ask one, then spend the rest of the interview asking you about your past job history. Your best defense is to know what your ethics are and go with how you honestly feel. There is no one right answer. If the board doesn't like what they hear then you may be grilled intensely about your answer; however, you should not assume that you've given a bad answer if the board does begin questioning you more intensely. Boards have more than one reason for hammering away at you, and it's never safe to assume why they are doing it.

Keep in mind, too, that it's not uncommon for one board member to be assigned the task of trying to get under an applicant's skin. The purpose of this is to see if the applicant rattles easily under pressure or loses his or her temper when baited. The person assigned this task is not hard to spot. He or she will be the one to ask questions such as: "Why in the world would we want to hire someone like YOU?"

Expect boards to jump on every discrepancy they hear and pick apart some of your comments—all because they want to see how you handle pressure. Not all departments designate a person to perform this function, but someone is usually prepared to slip into this role during the interview.

#### *Role-Play Situations*

Answering tough questions is stressful enough, but doing it under role-play conditions is even tougher. Agencies are using this technique more and more frequently in the oral board interview. A board member will instruct you to pretend you are a law enforcement agent and ask you to act out your verbal and/or physical responses. For example:

BOARD MEMBER: "Mr. Jones, I want you to pretend that you are a police officer and you are chasing a fleeing suspect. The suspect is running from you now and I want you to stand up and instruct him to stop by yelling: 'Freeze! Police!' "

Board members may set up more elaborate role-playing scenes for you. Try to enter these situations with a willingness to participate. Most people are aware that you are not a professional actor or actress, so they are not looking for Academy Award-winning performances. Do the best you can. Role-playing is used heavily in almost all police academies and training situations today, so expect to do a lot of it during your training as a law enforcement professional. Shy, reserved people may have difficulty with this kind of interaction. Practice how you'd handle these scenes.

## The Psychological Exam

Law enforcement work is one of the most stressful occupations in the world, and it is in your best interest and that of your future employers to weed out applicants who are unsuited for the job. While no one can guarantee that a given individual won't crack in a stressful situation, law enforcement agencies need to eliminate those applicants with underlying instabilities, choosing only those who will be able to deal with the job in healthy ways. The evaluation is also used to give agencies a little insight into your personality, your habits, and other factors. You may encounter oral evaluations, written ones like the Minnesota Multiphasic Personality Inventory (MMPI), or a combination of both.

When taking an exam like the MMPI, the idea is to relax, answer honestly, and not give answers that you think will present you only in the best light. Dr. Bradstreet's advice for both written psychological exams and oral exams is:

> Applicants try to make themselves appear to walk on water by answering all of the questions to appear the most virtuous. The idea of trying to look so good is not a good idea. People who are candid about their strengths and weaknesses do the best.

Oral psychological interviews are usually conducted by a psychologist or psychiatrist employed by, or contracting with, the hiring agency. This person may ask you questions about your schooling, jobs, habits, hobbies, and family relationships. Since there's such a broad range of things you could be asked about, there's really no way to prepare. In fact, the psychologist may be more interested in the way you answer questions—whether you come across as open, forthright, and honest—than in the answers you give.

## The Medical Examination

This part of the process will usually come at the end, after a conditional offer of employment. The exam itself is nothing unusual; it will be just like any other thorough physical exam. The doctor may be on the staff of the hiring agency or someone outside of the department with his or her own private practice. Your blood pressure, temperature, weight, and height will be measured; your heart and lungs will be listened to, ears and nose checked, and limbs examined. You will also have to donate a little blood to be analyzed.

A critical part of the exam is the vision test. Most law enforcement officers must have vision no worse than 20/200, corrected to 20/20, with normal functional color vision. This requirement can vary slightly from position to position, so if your uncorrected vision is not 20/20, check with the agency you're applying to about their standards. Because some of these tests have to be sent out to a lab, you won't know the results of the physical exam right away. You will be notified as soon as the test results are known.

Drug screening is usually conducted at the same time the medical exam is administered, but this can be done earlier in the process. Use of illegal drugs, of course, will disqualify you immediately from the process. If the test comes back positive because of a prescription drug you used, the department can ask you about it, but cannot use the condition for which the drug is prescribed to reject you, because of the Americans with Disabilities Act (ADA).

Depending on the agency to which you applied, you may have to wait weeks, months, or even more than a year to hear whether you will be offered a position.

While you're waiting, you might find support and encouragement from others who are going through a similar situation. There are a number of law enforcement websites (see Appendix A) which offer chat capabilities and message postings. Recent messages posted at police@groups.com concern the application process, how to deal with the wait, and whether to keep looking for other positions. The participants, ranging from seasoned professionals to rookies to recent applicants, were eager to offer each other support and advice.

## INSIDE TRACK

**Who:** Jorge Marquez
**What:** Supervisory Border Patrol Agent
**Where:** Imperial Beach Station, San Diego, CA
**How Long:** Eight years

The U.S. Border Patrol is the mobile, uniformed enforcement arm of the Immigration and Naturalization Service responsible for protecting our nation's border and protecting lives. Being a Border Patrol Agent is the kind of job that challenges you on every level—physically and mentally.

I am a Supervisory Border Patrol Agent with the U.S. Border Patrol. I became interested in the Border Patrol after hearing stories from a friend who was an Agent. I did a "ride-along" one night and enjoyed it so much that I started the application process the very next day. I've now been a Border Patrol agent for over eight years.

What I like most about my job is the diversity. We change shifts frequently and alternate between working days, evenings, and nights. I could go from patrolling the city streets one day to patrolling the backcountry and mountains the next to walking trails on foot. The Border Patrol also gives us many different resources to do our job. I rode on the horse patrol unit for two years without any prior experience with horses. We also have ATV units and bicycle units. In the more remote parts of the country, agents use motorcycles and snowmobiles.

An Agent's day usually starts with a muster. This is where we receive our area of assignment, our vehicle and any special equipment we might need. The Watch Commander also briefs us on any activity from the prior shift that may affect us or any change in operations. Then, it's off to the field where we'll do "sign-cutting" and tracking, patrolling and observing, or whatever our assignment calls for. The shift is eight hours long, but may last longer. Luckily, the extra hours we work are included in our pay.

Now, as a supervisor, I still do all the things that a regular agent does, and more. I make the assignment schedules. I schedule the days off and vacations for the agents. I also handle any special situations that occur in the field.

The Border Patrol has changed dramatically since I first joined. The Border Patrol has been hiring a lot of new agents, and with more agents we are better able to accomplish our mission of protecting the nation's borders. We now have more hi-tech equipment such as FLIR equipped helicopters. FLIR is an infrared system that allows helicopter pilots to see the ground clearly at night. We also have night-scopes mounted on trucks. These allow agents to see people at night from long distances by picking up the heat of their bodies.

If you are interested in the Border Patrol, I recommend you stay in good shape because it can be very physically demanding at times. Though demanding, it is one of the best jobs you'll ever have. There is also great potential for promotion if you work hard.

# Appendix A

## A Guide to Using the Internet

**THERE IS** no better tool for your career search than the Internet. The resources available are so wide that there is virtually nothing you can't find there. Law enforcement sites range from those maintained by local, state, and federal agencies to private ones that give just one law enforcement professional's insights. There are also chat rooms and message boards for contacting men and women who are also looking to work in the field. The key to successfully navigating the Internet is to know how to find what you are looking for.

This appendix will give you guidelines for conducting searches, as well as lists of sites worth visiting. Be aware that almost every day, new sites are created, so you should not think of this appendix as a finite list. Use your investigative skills to get the information you want and need.

### WWW: WHAT IT IS AND WHAT'S ON IT

If you aren't already familiar with some of the terminology, the Internet was created as a defense project, and has since become the world's largest computer network. Through the Internet, you can access the World Wide Web, a multimedia application that combines video, graphics, text, and sound. On the Web, you'll find millions of sites sponsored by various organizations and individuals.

Police and sheriff's departments, state troopers, and government agencies like the FBI, are discovering the advantages of posting information on their websites. Some agencies not only provide general information about their departments, but they also have their entire application process available for your inspection. You can even request applications and apply for many positions while online.

Andrea Richeson, a librarian for the State of Texas Technology Information Center, has advice for law enforcement job hunters:

> Ask a librarian for help! Even if your community does not have online access, you can probably get help and maybe even online access from county, state, federal, college, and university libraries. Look in your phone book's blue pages for contact information. Librarians can help you learn how to use the computer and/or print resources to help you find the information you need. If you are doing the searching yourself, the easiest way to gather information about law enforcement sites is to use search engines. Once you start pulling up websites with search engines, you'll see that they are linked to other law enforcement sites, and you'll be able to go on from there.

## Conducting Searches

To find what you are looking for, log onto search engine sites such as Yahoo.com, and Altavista.com. Yahoo, for instance, has categories from which to choose, so you can click on "Government," then "Law," then "Law Enforcement." The Law Enforcement category has a number of subcategories, including Employment, Law Enforcement Departments, S.W.A.T., and Web Directories. The Departments subcategory is further divided into Police and Sheriff Departments, each of which will give you links to hundreds of agencies. The Employment subcategory will give you links to many of the sites listed below, along with hundreds of others. You can also conduct your own search right from the first page of search sites. Each one is a little different, so click on "advanced searches," and read about the proper way to type in what you are looking for. For example, if you want sites that contain an exact phrase, such as "law enforcement career," you need to enclose the phrase in quotes. If you have just a few key words, and they can appear anywhere in the document, you may have to use a plus sign in front of each of the words. Each site has good instructions, which are easy to follow.

Once you have found and logged onto a site, you will find links to other sites. There are a number of law enforcement sites that can link you to career information, educational information, message boards, state and federal agencies, news about law enforcement, and so on. Other sites are much more specific, and while they may contain a few links, they are much narrower in scope than the larger "clearinghouse"-type sites.

Throughout this book, we have listed many websites that provide valuable information. Many of them appear again below, along with a number of other sites, to provide you with one list to get your search started.

## General Law Enforcement Sites

These are "clearinghouses," providing links to many other sites and containing a wide range of information. You can find employment listings, bookstores, message boards, relevant news items, educational information, support for officers and their families, and even auctions of law enforcement-related memorabilia.

www.leolinks.com

A comprehensive law enforcement site includes links to law enforcement agencies, officer's homes pages, and other police-related sites.

www.officer.com

Launched by a young police officer in 1995, this site contains links to law-enforcement related sites and also posts national articles concerning law enforcement.

www.policeguide.com

"Your Guide to Cop Culture" has eclectic offerings including a Free FBI Records Search, Police Supply Advertisers, Police Jobs, Free Classified Ads, and a SWAT Directory.

www.pimacc.pima.edu/dps/police.htm

"The most complete list of Law Enforcement Agencies on the Web" contains links for over 3,800 criminal justice agencies.

www.copsonline.com
The "Interactive Police Website" contains resources on police videos, free police websites, police books, and other related services.

www.policeone.com
A general site providing links and information to law enforcement career training and possibilities as well as to related articles and products for purchase.

## Education-related Sites

These sites allow you to input information about yourself and search for colleges, internships, and the money to pay for them based on your preferences. You can also find guides to help you to determine those preferences.

*Test Prep*

www.learnatest.com
Offers effective online practice tests for police officers, state police, and TEA with instant scoring and personalized analysis. Also offers career advice and test taking tips.

*Internships*

www.internships.com
Contains general and regional guides for internship possibilities nationwide.

www.internjobs.com
Provides a national database of internships. Students and recent graduates can search the database by keyword or location and post online resumes for employers to view.

*Scholarships*

www.gripvision.com
A free online magazine, "written and edited entirely by teenagers," includes information and a search engine on scholarships, financial aid, grants, loans, and colleges.

www.scholarships.com
"The Largest and Fastest Free College Scholarship Search on the Internet" allows users to create a personalized profile comparing their scholarship needs to a database of over 600,000 college scholarships award programs.

*Financial aid*

www.finaid.org
"The SmartStudent™ Guide to Financial Aid" lists and explains eligibility for student loans, scholarships, military, and other types of programs.

www.fedmoney.org
A comprehensive list of all U.S. government programs benefiting students including information on grants, loans, scholarships, fellowships, and traineeships.

## Law Enforcement Employment Sites

These sites range from offering listings of available jobs with contact information, to selling career guides, to allowing you to post your resume so that agencies that are hiring can contact you.

www.policeemployment.com
Offers a wide variety of guides and videos on state and federal police employment as well as law enforcement agency and hiring links.

www.onpatrol.com/employ.html
"The Premier Law Enforcement Magazine" lists law enforcement job opportunities nationwide.

www.lawenforcementjob.com
Contains employment information on over 2,500 law-enforcement departments and agencies.

www.psrjobs.com/lawrecru.htm
A subscription site giving weekly updates on recruitment information from law enforcement agencies nationwide.

www.policecareer.com
A listing of vacancies in law enforcement positions nationwide.

www.statetrooper.net
An e-mail service offering the United States Law Enforcement Career Guide providing career information on law-enforcement agencies nationwide.

www.jobs4police.com
"The Only Effective Guide for Law Enforcement!" offers information on law-enforcement training programs and job listings.

www.lejobs.com
Contains information about agencies that are currently hiring for law enforcement and other support related positions.

## Other Sites and E-mail Addresses

www.police.trainingontheweb.com
Provides web-based course listings for post-academy training through Pegasus Online Campus.

police@egroups.com

www.communitypolicing.org
The Community Policing Consortium is a partnership of five leading police organizations in the United States committed to the development of community policing research and training and technical assistance.

# Appendix B

## FBI Field Offices

**THIS APPENDIX** contains a list of addresses, telephone numbers, and websites (if applicable) for the 56 FBI field offices in major U.S. cities and in Puerto Rico. Check with the location nearest you for recruiting information. The offices are listed alphabetically by city.

Federal Bureau of Investigation
200 McCarty Avenue
Albany, NY 12209
(518) 465-7551
www.fbi.gov/contact/fo/alfo/alfohome.htm

Federal Bureau of Investigation
Suite 300
415 Silver Avenue, Southwest
Albuquerque, NM 87102
(505) 224-2000
www.fbi.gov/contact/fo/aq/aqhome.htm

Federal Bureau of Investigation
101 East Sixth Avenue
Anchorage, AK 99501-2524
(907) 258-5322

Federal Bureau of Investigation
Suite 400
2635 Century Parkway, Northeast
Atlanta, GA 30345-3112
(404) 679-9000
www.fbi.gov/contact/fo/atlanta/index.htm

Federal Bureau of Investigation
7142 Ambassador Road
Baltimore, MD 21244-2754
(410) 265-8080
www.fbi.gov/contact/fo/balt/index.htm

Federal Bureau of Investigation
Room 1400
2121 8th Avenue N.
Birmingham, AL 35203-2396
(205) 326-6166
www.fbi.gov/contact/fo/birmingham/index.htm

Federal Bureau of Investigation
Suite 600
One Center Plaza
Boston, MA 02108
(617) 742-5533
www.fbi.gov/contact/fo/boston/boston.htm

Federal Bureau of Investigation
One FBI Plaza
Buffalo, NY 14202-2698
(716) 856-7800
www.fbi.gov/contact/fo/bffo/bffohome/htm

Federal Bureau of Investigation
Suite 900, Wachovia Building
400 South Tyron Street
Charlotte, NC 28285-0001
(704) 377-9200
www.fbi.gov/contact/fo/charlotte/ce_home.htm

Federal Bureau of Investigation
Room 905
E.M. Dirksen Federal Office Building
219 South Dearborn Street
Chicago, IL 60604-1702
(312) 431-1333
www.fbi.gov/contact/fo/chicago/index.htm

Federal Bureau of Investigation
Room 9000
550 Main Street
Cincinnati, Ohio 45202-8501
(513) 421-4310
www.fbi.gov/contact/fo/ci/index.htm

Federal Bureau of Investigation
Room 3005
Federal Office Building
1240 East 9th Street
Cleveland, OH 44199-9912
(216) 522-1400
www.fbi.gov/contact/fo/cleveland/clevelan1.htm

Federal Bureau of Investigation
151 Westpark Boulevard
Columbia, SC 29210-3857
(803) 551-4200

Federal Bureau of Investigation
Suite 300
1801 North Lamar
Dallas, TX 75202-1795
(214) 720-2200
www.fbi.gov/contact/fo/dl/dallas.htm

Federal Bureau of Investigation
Federal Office Building, Room 1823
1961 Stout Street, 18th Floor
Denver, CO 80294-1823
(303) 629-7171
www.fbi.gov/contact/fo/denver/denver.htm

Federal Bureau of Investigation
26th. Floor, P. V. McNamara FOB
477 Michigan Avenue
Detroit, MI 48226
(313) 965-2323
www.fbi.gov/contact/fo/detroit/default/htm

Federal Bureau of Investigation
660 S. Mesa Hills Drive
El Paso, TX 79912-5533
(915) 832-5000

Federal Bureau of Investigation
Room 4-230, Kalanianaole FOB
300 Ala Moana Boulevard
Honolulu, HI 96850-0053
(808) 521-1411

Federal Bureau of Investigation
2500 East TC Jester
Houston, TX 77008-1300
(713) 693-5000
www.fbi.gov/contact/fo/ho/houston.htm

Federal Bureau of Investigation
Room 679, FOB
575 North Pennsylvania Street
Indianapolis, IN 46204-1585
(317) 639-3301

Federal Bureau of Investigation
Room 1553, FOB
100 West Capitol Street
Jackson, MS 39269-1601
(601) 948-5000
www.fbi.gov/contact/fo/jackson/jackson.htm

Federal Bureau of Investigation
Suite 200
7820 Arlington Expressway
Jacksonville, FL 32211-7499
(904) 721-1211

Federal Bureau of Investigation
1300 Summit
Kansas City, MO 64105-1362
(816) 512-8200
www.fbi.gov/contact/fo/kc/kcpage.htm

Federal Bureau of Investigation
Suite 600, John J. Duncan FOB
710 Locust Street
Knoxville, TN 37902-2537
(423) 544-0751
www.fbi.gov/contact/fo/kx/knoxhome.htm

Federal Bureau of Investigation
John Lawrence Bailey Building
700 East Charleston Boulevard
Las Vegas, NV 89104-1545
(702) 385-1281

Federal Bureau of Investigation
Suite 200
Two Financial Centre
10825 Financial Centre Parkway
Little Rock, AK 72211-3552
(501) 221-9100
www.fbi.gov/contact/fo/lr/main.htm

Federal Bureau of Investigation
Suite 1700, FOB
11000 Wilshire Boulevard
Los Angeles, CA 90024-3672
(310) 477-6565
www.fbi.gov/contact/fo/la/main.htm

Federal Bureau of Investigation
Room 500
600 Martin Luther King Jr. Place
Louisville, KY 40202-2231
(502) 583-3941
www.fbi.gov/contact/fo/louisville/fbilou.htm

Federal Bureau of Investigation
Suite 3000, Eagle Crest Bldg.
225 North Humphreys Blvd.
Memphis, TN 38120-2107
(901) 747-4300
www.fbi.gov/contact/fo/memphis/default.htm

Federal Bureau of Investigation
16320 Northwest Second Avenue
North Miami Beach, FL 33169-6508
(305) 944-9101
www.fbi.gov/contact/fo/mb/index.htm

Federal Bureau of Investigation
Suite 600
330 East Kilbourn Avenue
Milwaukee, WI 53202-6627
(414) 276-4684

Federal Bureau of Investigation
Suite 1100
111 Washington Avenue, South
Minneapolis, MN 55401-2176
(612) 376-3200
www.fbi.gov/contact/fo/minn/home.htm

Federal Bureau of Investigation
One St. Louis Centre
1 St. Louis Street, 3rd Floor
Mobile, AL 36602-3930
(334) 438-3674
www.fbi.gov/contact/fo/mobile/home.htm

Federal Bureau of Investigation
1 Gateway Center, 22nd Floor
Newark, NJ 07102-9889
(973) 622-5613

Federal Bureau of Investigation
Room 535, FOB
150 Court Street
New Haven, CT 06510-2020
(203) 777-6311

Federal Bureau of Investigation
2901 Leon C. Simon Drive
New Orleans, LA 70126
(504) 816-3000
www.fbi.gov/contact/fo/neworlean/index.htm

Federal Bureau of Investigation
26 Federal Plaza, 23rd Floor
New York, NY 10278-0004
(212) 384-1000
www.fbi.gov/contact/fo/nyfo/nyfohome.htm

Federal Bureau of Investigation
150 Corporate Boulevard
Norfolk, VA 23502-4999
(757) 455-0100
www.fbi.gov/contact/fo/norfolk/home.htm

Federal Bureau of Investigation
3301 West Memorial Drive
Oklahoma City, OK 73134
(405) 290-7770

Federal Bureau of Investigation
10755 Burt Street
Omaha, NE 68114-2000
(402) 493-8688

Federal Bureau of Investigation
8th Floor
William J. Green Jr. FOB
600 Arch Street
Philadelphia, PA 19106
(215) 418-4000
www.fbi.gov/contact/fo/ph/phila1a.htm

Federal Bureau of Investigation
Suite 400
201 East Indianola Avenue
Phoenix, AZ 85012-2080
(602) 279-5511
www.fbi.gov/contact/fo/phnx/default.htm

Federal Bureau of Investigation
Suite 300
U.S. Post Office Building
700 Grant Street
Pittsburgh, PA 15219-1906
(412) 471-2000
www.fbi.gov/contact/fo/pt/pitmain.htm

Federal Bureau of Investigation
Suite 400, Crown Plaza Building
1500 Southwest 1st Avenue
Portland, OR 97201-5828
(503) 224-4181
www.fbi.gov/contact/fo/pd/portlnd.htm

Federal Bureau of Investigation
111 Greencourt Road
Richmond, VA 23228-4948
(804) 261-1044
www.fbi.gov/contact/fo/richmond/default.htm

Federal Bureau of Investigation
4500 Orange Grove Avenue
Sacramento, CA 95841-4205
(916) 481-9110
www.fbi.gov/contact/fo/sc/fbisc/htm

Federal Bureau of Investigation
2222 Market Street
St. Louis, MO 63103-2516
(314) 231-4324
www.fbi.gov/contact/fo/sl/home.htm

Federal Bureau of Investigation
Suite 1200, 257 Towers Bldg.
257 East, 200 South
Salt Lake City, UT 84111-2048
(801) 579-1400
www.fbi.gov/contact/fo/saltlake/index.htm

Federal Bureau of Investigation
Suite 200
U.S. Post Office Courthouse Bldg.
615 East Houston Street
San Antonio, TX 78205-9998
(210) 225-6741
www.fbi.gov/contact/fo/sanant/sanant.htm

Federal Bureau of Investigation
Federal Office Building
9797 Aero Drive
San Diego, CA 92123-1800
(619) 565-1255
www.fbi.gov/contact/fo/sandiego/index.htm

Federal Bureau of Investigation
450 Golden Gate Avenue, 13th Floor
San Francisco, CA 94102-9523
(415) 553-7400

Federal Bureau of Investigation
Room 526, U.S. Federal Bldg.
150 Carlos Chardon Avenue
Hato Rey
San Juan, Puerto Rico 00918-1716
(787) 754-6000

Federal Bureau of Investigation
Room 710
915 Second Avenue
Seattle, WA 98174-1096
(206) 622-0460
www.fbi.gov/contact/fo/seattle/default.htm

Federal Bureau of Investigation
Suite 400
400 West Monroe Street
Springfield, IL 62704-1800
(217) 522-9675
www.fbi.gov/contact/fo/si/spfldfbi/htm

Federal Bureau of Investigation
Room 610, FOB
500 Zack Street
Tampa, FL 33602-3917
(813) 273-4566
www.fbi.gov/contact/fo/tampa/tampa_home.htm

Federal Bureau of Investigation
Washington Metropolitan Field Office
601 4th Street, N. W.
Washington, D.C. 20535-0002
(202) 252-2000

# Appendix C

## Additional Published Resources

**THIS APPENDIX** contains a list of useful books that will give you more specific advice on areas with which you may need help during your career planning and job search. For additional information on the topics discussed in this book, refer to the following reading lists, which are organized by subject.

### Colleges

*Barron's Profiles of American Colleges: with Windows and Mac Software*. Barron's Educational Series, Inc., 1998.

The College Board. *The College Handbook 1998*. 35th ed. College Entrance Exam Board, 1997.

Custard, Edward T. and The Princeton Review. *The Best 331 Colleges, 2000 Edition*. New York: Random House, 1999.

Fiske, Edward B. *The Fiske Guide to Colleges 2000*. Crown Publishing Group, 1999.

*Peterson's Guide to Two-Year Colleges 1998: The Only Guide to More than 1,500 Community and Junior Colleges*. Princeton, NJ: Peterson's, 1997.

Ordovensky, Pat. *College Planning for Dummies*. IDG Books Worldwide, 1999.

Yale Daily News. *The Insider's Guide to the Colleges*. St. Martin's Press, 1999.

### Financial Aid

Chany, Kalman A., and Geoff Martz. *Student Advantage Guide to Paying for College, 1997 Edition*. New York: Random House, The Princeton Review, 1997.

College School Service. *College Costs & Financial Aid Handbook*. 18th ed. New York: The College Entrance Examination Board, 1998.

Cook, Melissa L. *College Student's Handbook to Financial Assistance and Planning*. Moonbeam Publications, Inc., 1991.

Davis, Kristen. *Financing College: How to Use Savings, Financial Aid, Scholarships, and Loans to Afford the School of Your Choice*. Washington, DC: Random House, 1996.

Davis, Hern, and Joyce Lain Kennedy. *College Financial Aid for Dummies*. IDG Books Worldwide, 1999.

See also Scholarships section, below.

## Job Hunting

Baird, Brian N. *The Internship, Practicum, and Field Placement Handbook: A Guide for the Helping Professions*. Upper Saddle River, NJ: Prentice Hall, 1999.

Bernstein, Sara T., and Kathleen M. Savage, eds. *Vocational Careers Sourcebook*. New York: Gale Research, International Thomson Publishers, 1996.

Bureau of Labor Statistics. *Dictionary of Occupational Titles*. 2 vols. 4th ed. Bureau of Labor Statistics, 1991.

Bureau of Labor Statistics. *Occupational Outlook Handbook*, 1996–1997.

Cubbage, Sue A., and Marcia P. Williams. *The 1996 National Job Hotline Directory*. New York: McGraw-Hill, 1996.

DeLucia, Robert C., and Thomas J. Doyle. *Career Planning in Criminal Justice*. Cincinnati: Anderson Publishing Co., 1994.

Eyre, Vivian V. *Great Interview: Successful Strategies for Getting Hired*. New York: LearningExpress, 2000

Harr, J. Scott, J.D., and Karen M. Hess, Ph.D. *Seeking Employment in Criminal Justice and Related Fields*. Belmont, CA: Wadsworth/Thomson Learning, 2000.

Henry, Stuart, ed. *Inside Jobs: A Realistic Guide to Criminal Justice Careers for College Graduates*. Salem, Wisconsin: Sheffield Publishing Co., 1994.

The Justice Research Association. *Your Criminal Justice Career: A Guidebook*. Upper Saddle River, NJ: Prentice Hall, 2000.

Rich, Jason. *Great Resume: Get Noticed, Get Hired.* New York: LearningExpress, 2000.

Sonneblick, Carol, Kim Crabbe, and Michaele Basciano. *Job Hunting Made Easy.* New York: LearningExpress, 1997.

Stephens, W. Richard, Jr. *Careers in Criminal Justice.* Needham Heights, MA: Allyn and Bacon, 1999.

Taylor, Dorothy. *Jumpstarting Your Career: An Internship Guide for Criminal Justice.* Upper Saddle River, NJ: Prentice Hall, Inc., 1999.

## Law Enforcement Exams

*Corrections Officer: Florida.* New York: LearningExpress, 1996.

*Corrections Officer: New Jersey.* New York: LearningExpress, 1996.

*Corrections Officer: New York.* New York: LearningExpress, 1996.

*Corrections Officer: Texas.* New York: LearningExpress, 1996.

*Police Officer Exam: California.* New York: LearningExpress, 1996.

*Police Officer Exam: Chicago.* New York: LearningExpress, 1997.

*Police Officer Exam: Florida.* New York: LearningExpress, 1996.

*Police Officer Exam: New York City.* New York: LearningExpress, 1998.

*Police Officer Exam: The Midwest.* New York: LearningExpress, 1997.

*Police Officer Exam: The South.* New York: LearningExpress, 1997.

*State Police Exam: California.* New York: LearningExpress, 1996.

*State Police Exam: New Jersey.* New York: LearningExpress, 1997.

*State Police Exam: New York.* New York: LearningExpress, 1996.

*State Police Exam: Texas.* New York: LearningExpress, 1996.

## Scholarship Guides

Cassidy, Daniel J. *The Scholarship Book 2000: The Complete Guide to Private-Sector Scholarships, Fellowships, Grants, and Loans for the Undergraduate.* Englewood Cliffs, NJ: Prentice Hall, 1999.

*Peterson's Scholarships, Grants and Prizes 2000.* Peterson's Guides, 1999.

Ragins, Marianne. *Winning Scholarships for College: An Insider's Guide.* New York: Henry Holt & Co., 1994.

*Scholarships, Grants & Prizes: Guide to College Financial Aid from Private Sources*. Princeton, NJ: Peterson's, 1998.

Schwartz, John. *College Scholarships and Financial Aid*. New York: Simon & Schuster, Macmillan, 1995.

Schlacter, Gail, and R. David Weber. *Scholarships 2000*. New York: Kaplan, 1999.

## Studying

Chesla, Elizabeth. *Read Better, Remember More*. New York: LearningExpress, 1997.

Chesla, Elizabeth. *Reading Comprehension Success in 20 Minutes a Day*. 2nd ed. New York: LearningExpress, 1998.

Coman, Marcia J., and Kathy L. Heavers. *How to Improve Your Study Skills*. 2nd ed. Lincolnwood, IL: NTC Publishing, 1998.

Fry, Ron. *Ron Fry's How to Study Program*. 4th ed. New Jersey: Career Press, 1996.

Meyers, Judith N. *Vocabulary and Spelling Success in 20 Minutes a Day*. 2nd ed. New York: LearningExpress, 1998.

Robinovitz, Judith. *Practical Math Success in 20 Minutes a Day*. 2nd ed. New York: LearningExpress, 1998.

Silver, Theodore M.D., J.D. *The Princeton Review Study Smart: Hands-On Nuts-and-Bolts Techniques for Earning Higher Grades*. New York: Villard Books, 1995.

Wood, Gail. *How to Study*. New York: LearningExpress, 1997.

## Test Help

Kaplan. *ACT: Powerful Strategies to Help You Score Higher: 1998 ed.* New York: Simon & Schuster, 1997.

*ASVAB: Armed Services Vocational Aptitude Battery*. New York: LearningExpress, 1997.

College Board. *The College Board: 10 real SATs*. New York: College Entrance Exam Board, 1997.

Katyman, John, and Adam Robinson. *Cracking the SAT & PSAT, 1998 Edition*. New York: Random House, The Princeton Review, 1997.

Meyers, Judith N. *The Secrets of Taking Any Test*. New York: LearningExpress, 1997.

Previous edition SAT and ACT test preparation books should also be available at your local library.

## Miscellaneous

The Criminal Justice Distance Learning Consortium. *The Definitive Guide to Criminal Justice and Criminology on the World Wide Web*. Upper Saddle River, NJ: Prentice Hall, 1999.